CONTENTS

INTRODUCTION

THE ENGLISHMAN'S reputation as a lover abroad is
not an impressive one. Natural reticence is to blame
as well as a chronic inability to express himself in
any other language but his own. He cannot rise to
the hot breath and the passionate gesture of his con-
tinental counterpart; his eyes do not flash, his
bosom does not heave; his approach is without
nicety, lacking the suggestive subtlety of the French-
man, the gay bottom-pinching abandon of the
Italian or the smouldering intensity of the Spaniard.

How, then is he to hold his own in a foreign land
—especially when he is limited (as he usually is) to
a brief sortie which must begin, flourish and end in a
summer's holiday fortnight?

This little book may perhaps help him. He should
remember that remarks that verge on the outrageous
are more easily forgiven in the foreigner he has
temporarily become. Not only will his atrocious
accent give a certain endearing softening to the
impact of the words here set down for his use, but,
being only half-understood by his fair acquaintance,
they may well give rise to just the right climate of
questing that can flower into an understanding, a

4

The LOVER'S Dictionary

****

How to chat up a bird in five languages

WARD LOCK LIMITED · LONDON

To James

Uniform with this volume:
THE INSULT DICTIONARY

This edition published in Great Britain in 1979 by Ward Lock Limited, 116 Baker Street, London W1M 2BB, a Pentos Company

ISBN 0-7063-5827-9

Printed in Great Britain by
Lowe & Brydone Printers Limited
Thetford, Norfolk

quickening of interest and, eventually, to a holiday well spent . . .

Anyway, he can but try; he need not yearn with a tied tongue, for here are the words to meet any romantic situation. And, even if the law of averages works against him and he is rewarded with ten face-slaps to every responsive heart-beat, he may well consider this fair return for his love-labour and something to remember in the lean and slippered years that lie ahead.

The Editors make no apology for having addressed this phrase-book to the needs of the young male; they feel that girls stretching out their lovely arms for beaux on the Continent will need no fine phrases or dictionary definitions—just a course in Judo, which is outside the scope of THE LOVER'S DICTIONARY.

NOTES ON PRONUNCIATION
by the translators

FRENCH. Gallic polysyllabic fluency comes hard to the Anglo-Saxon, accustomed as he is to being a man of few words. French vowels, uttered with the force of a minor explosion, come hard too. And in the state of high passion in which we hope readers of this book will find themselves, there will be neither time nor inclination to ponder deeply on pronunciation. We have, therefore, altered some French sounds to try to make them similar to English vowels. (If said pretty quickly, they almost sound like the real thing.) Here are a few notes that will help in reading the phonetic version:

Where there is 'u' in French, or 'ure', the u has been replaced by i. This must be pronounced as in 'bit' and not as in 'bite'.

The French 'j' has been translated by 'sh', but this must be pronounced fairly lightly. The word 'garage' has this sound.

The 'e', 'eu' and 'eur' sounds are expressed as 'er' or 'ehr'. Quite easy, if you lengthen them a bit. 'Euse' has been put as 'ehrz'.

Liaisons have been put in as being part of the word, in almost every case.

The 'ail' sound was the hardest to translate—'ay' dare not be used in case it was pronounced as in 'may'—so, it was decided to use 'aee' or 'a'ee'—but the ee must not be stressed.

'En', 'em', 'in', 'im', 'ein' and 'un' have all been translated by 'an' or 'am'. You can get away with it in the heat of the moment.

'Oi' by 'w', of course. Easy.

Finally, all would-be French speakers are reminded that in this delightful language all words are stressed on the last syllable, whatever the length.

GERMAN. The German double letter 'ß' is replaced here by 'ss'. Other usages are:

ch :	pronounce hard as in loch
g :	pronounce hard as in good
i :	read always short as in 'fit'
y :	like 'fly'
ao :	as in 'owl'

ITALIAN. The Italian translator has produced his own system of phonetics, which should stand the one-language Englishman in good stead. He reminds you that in Italian every vowel io pronounced.

SPANISH. *á* or *ah* is pronounced as the English *a* in *car*. (Never like *all, dare, gave.*)
é or *eh* is always like the English *e* in *set, let, wet*. (Never like *me, here, become.*)
ó or *oh* has the sound of English *o* in *lord* or English *aw* in *law*. (Never like *old, go, ago.*)
i has the sound of *i* in *bit*. (Never of *I, mine island.*)
y has the sound of *y* in *yes, yawn*, or the *e* in *me*. (Never like *my, by, cry.*)
th has the sound of English *th* in *thing*. (Never of *the, that, this.*)

SPECIAL NOTE. As in *THE INSULT DICTIONARY* the translations are intended to give local equivalents or to express the same understandable idea, not to give mere literal equivalents that may mean nothing to the other person.

7

Please excuse me—wrong cabin.

O, Verzeihung—falsche Kabine!

(O, fertsy-oong—faalshe cabine.)

Actually I'm travelling incognito.

Ehrlich gestanden, ich reise inkognito.

(Erlish geshtaanden, ish ryze incognito.)

I thought you needed steadying.

Ich dachte, ich sollte Sie festhalten.

(Ish daachte, ish zolte zi festhaalten.)

Where am I? I must have been sleep-walking.

Wo bin ich? Nachtwandele ich?

(Vo bin ish? Naacht-vaandle ish?)

Honestly, these pills are just for sea-sickness.

Wirklich, diese Pillen sind nur gegen Seekrankheit.

(Virklish, dise pillen zind noor gaygen zaykraankhyt.)

FRENCH	ITALIAN	SPANISH
Oh, pardon! Je me suis trompé de cabine. *(Oh pardon! Sherm swee trompay der cabeen.)*	Scusi, ho sbagliato cabina. *(Skoo-zy oh sbah-lee-ah-toh kah-bee-nah.)*	Perdone. Me he equivocado de camarote. *(Perdóneh. Meh eh ekkiboccádoh deh kahmahróteh.)*
A vrai dire, je voyage incognito. *(Ar vray deer, sher vwahyash anconeeto.)*	Veramente viaggio in incognito. *(Veh-rah-menteh vee-ah-joh een in-koh-nee-toh.)*	Realmente, viajo de incógnito. *(Reh-alménteh, beeyáhho deh eencógnitoh.)*
J'ai cru que vous aviez besoin d'aide. *(Shay cri ker voo zavyay berzwan daid.)*	Credevo che avesse bisogno di appoggio. *(Creh-deh-voh keh ah-vehsseh bee-zoh-nee-oh dee appóh-joh.)*	Creí que iba a caerse. *(Kreh-ee ké eebah ah kahérseh.)*
Où suis-je? J'ai dû avoir encore une crise de somnanbulisme. *(Oo sweesh? Shay di ahvwar ankor in creez der somnanbileezm.)*	Dove sono? Devo essere sonnambulo. *(Doh-veh soh-noh? Deh-voh esseh-reh son-nahm-boo-loh.)*	¿Dónde estoy? ¡Debo ser sonámbulo! *(Dóndeh stóy? Déboh sér sonámbooloh!)*
Je vous jure que ces pilules sont contre le mal de mer. *(Sher voo shir ker say peelil son contr ler mal der mair.)*	L'assicuro, queste pillole sono soltanto per il mal di mare. *(Lahs-see-koo-roh, kwehsteh pilloh-leh soh•noh per eel mahl dee mah-reh.)*	¡Palabra! Estas píldoras son sólo contra el mareo. *(Pahlábrah! Éstass peeldórass són sóloh kóntrah él mahréh-oh.)*

ON BOARD SHIP

There's a much better view from my cabin.

Von meiner Kabine hat man eine bessere Aussicht.

(Fon myner cabine haat maan yne bessere aosisht.)

It's my birthday, do have just one drink with me.

Trinken Sie doch wenigstens ein Gläschen mit mir—heute ist mein Geburtstag.

(Trinken zi doch venigstens yn glays-shen mit mir—hoyte ist myn geboortstag.)

ON THE PLANE

I'm sorry, I was trying to fasten my seat-belt.

O, Verzeihung, ich wollte meinen Sicherheitsgurt festschnallen.

(O, fertsy-oong, ish volte mynen zisherhyts-goort festshnallen.)

Do you mind holding my hand? I'm frightened at take-off.

Würden Sie bitte meine Hand halten? Ich habe Angst vor dem Aufsteigen.

(Vuerden zi bitte myne haand haalten? Ish haabe aangst for daym aofshtygen.)

FRENCH	ITALIAN	SPANISH
Venez dans ma cabine, on a une de ces vues . . . !	Dalla mia cabina c'è una vista molto piú bella.	Hay mejores vistas desde mi camarote.
(Vernay dan ma cabeen, on ar in der say vi . . . !)	*(Dahl-lah mee-ah kah-bee-nah cheh oo-nah vee-stah mohl-toh pew bel-lah.)*	*(Áy mehhóress beestass dés-deh mee kahmahróteh.)*
C'est mon anniversaire, venez donc boire juste un verre avec moi.	Prenda qualcosa da bere con me—è il mio comple-anno.	Es mi cumpleaños. Venga a tomar un trago conmigo.
(Say mon aneevairsair, ver-nay donk bwar shist an vair aveck mwar.)	*(Prehn-dah kwal-koh-zah dah beh-reh kon meh—eh eel mee-oh kom-pleh-ahn-noh.)*	*(Ess mee koompleh-ányoss. Béngah ah tohmárr oon trágoh kón-meegoh.)*
Je m'excuse, j'essayais de boucler la ceinture.	Scusi, stavo cercando di allacciare la cintura del sedile.	Lo siento. Quería apretar mi cinturón de seguridad.
(Sher mexkiz, shessayay der booklay la santir.)	*(Skoo-zy, stah-voh cher-can-doh dee allah-chee-ah-reh lah cheen-too-rah dehl seh-dee-leh.)*	*(Loh seeyéntoh. Kehreeyàh aprehtárr mee thintoorón dé segooreedáth.)*
Gardez ma main dans la vôtre, je vous prie, je suis terrifié chaque fois que l'avion va décoller.	Le dispiace tenermi la mano? Ho tanta paura al momento del decollo.	¿Le importaría darme la mano? Me asusta mucho despegar.
(Garday ma man dan la votr, sher voo pree, sher swee terreefyay shack fwar ker lavyon va daicolay.)	*(Leh dee-spee-ah-cheh teh-ner-mee lah mah-noh? Oh tahn-tah pah-oo-rah ahl momentoh dehl deh-kol-loh.)*	*(Leh importareeya dármeh lá mánoh? Meh assoostah mootchoh despehgárr.)*

ON THE PLANE

I don't know anyone or where to go in ......

Ich kenne niemanden hier und weiss auch nicht, wo es 'lang geht.

(Ish kenne nimaanden heer oond vys aoch nisht, vo es laang gayt.)

Take the middle arm-rest out, it's more comfortable.

Nehmen Sie die Armlehne zwischen uns 'raus, das ist bequemer.

(Naymen zi di armlayne tsvishen oons 'raos, daas ist bequaymer.)

Try this air-sickness pill.

Probieren Sie 'mal diese Pillen, wenn Sie luftkrank werden.

(Probiren zi 'maal dise pillen, ven zi looftkraank verden.)

SOME USEFUL WORDS

Adorable.

Entzückend.
(Entsueckend.)

Irresistible.

Unwiderstehlich.
(Oonvider-shtaylish.)

FRENCH	ITALIAN	SPANISH

Je ne connais personne à
...... et je ne sais où aller.

*(Shern conay pairson ar
...... ay shern say oo
allay.)*

A ...... non conosco
nessuno, e non so proprio
dove andare.

*(Ah ...... non coh-noh-
skoh neh-soo-noh eh non soh
proh-preeoh doh-veh ahn-
dah-reh.)*

No conozco a nadie ni sé
donde ir en ......

*(Noh konóthkoh ah náddye
nee sé dóndeh eer én ......)*

Si on relevait l'accoudoir
du milieu, ce sera plus
confortable!

*(See on rehlvay lacoodwar
di meelyer, ser srah pli
confortahbl!)*

Togliamo il bracciolo di
mezzo—è tanto piú comodo
senza.

*(Toh-lee-ah-moh eel brah-
chee-oh-loh dee metzoh—
eh tahn-toh pew koh-moh-
doh sen-tzah.)*

Quite el apoyabrazos cen-
tral, se está más cómodo.

*(Keeteh él ahpóyah-bráthoss
zentrál, sé stá máss
kómodoh.)*

Prenez cette pilule, c'est
bon contre le mal de l'air.

*(Prehnay set peelil, say bon
contr ler mal der lair.)*

Provi questa pillola contro
il mal d'aria.

*(Proh-vee kwestah pilloh-la
cohn-troh eel mahl da-ree-
ah.)*

Tómese estas pastillas
contra el mareo.

*(Tómeh-seh éstass pastec-
llyass kóntrah él mahréh-oh.)*

Adorable.

(Addorahbl.)

Adorabile.

(Ahdor-ahbeeleh.)

Adorable.

(Adoráh-bleh.)

Irrésistible.

(Eerezeesteebl.)

Irresistibile.

(Irresist-eebee-leh.)

Irresistible.

(Irresistee-bleh.)

IN THE TRAIN

Excuse me, miss, is that seat taken?

Entschuldigen Sie, Fräulein, ist dieser Platz noch frei?

(Entshooldigen, zi, fräulyn, ist diser plaats noch fry?)

I'm so sorry, the train keeps rocking towards you.

Tut mir leid, aber der Zug schaukelt immer nach dieser Seite.

(Toot mir lyd, aaber der tsoog shaokelt immer naach diser syte.)

I hope you can squeeze an extra one in.

Da ist doch bestimmt noch eine kleine Lücke frei.

(Daa ist doch beshtimmt noch yne klyne luecke fry.)

You look too young to be travelling alone—are you sixteen yet?

Sie sind doch viel zu jung, um schon allein zu reisen. Sind Sie schon sechzehn?

(Zi zind doch fil tsoo yoong, oom shon allyn tsoo ryzen. Zind zi shon zayshtsayn?)

FRENCH	ITALIAN	SPANISH

Excusez-moi, s'il vous plaît, est-ce que cette place est prise?

(Exkizay-mwar, seel voo play, esker set plahs ay preez?)

Scusi signorina, è occupato quel posto?

(Skoo-zy see-nee-oh-ree-nah, eh ok-koo-pah-toh kwel poh-stoh?)

Perdone, señorita, ¿está ocupado este asiento?

(Perdónneh, senyoreetah, stá okoopádoh ésteh assyéntoh?)

Je m'excuse, mais je ne peux empêcher le mouvement du train de me jeter vers vous.

(Sher mexkiz, may shern perzampaishay ler moovman di tran der mer shertay vair voo.)

Mi scusi tanto ma è il movimento del treno che mi spinge contro di lei.

(Mee skoo-zy tan-toh mah eh eel moh-vee-men-toh dehl treh-noh keh mee speen-jeh kon-troh dee leh-ee.)

Lo siento, el tren se balancea hacia su lado.

(Loh seeyéntoh, él trén seh balanthéah áthiah soo ládoh.)

J'espère que vous voudrez bien vous serrer un peu pour me faire une petite place.

(Shaispair ker voo voodray byan voo serray an per poor mer fair in perteet plahs.)

Me lo fa un posticino piccolo piccolo?

(Meh loh fah oon poh-stee-chee-noh pick-koh-loh pick-koh-loh?)

Espero que pueda apretarse un poquito más.

(Spéroh ké pwéddah aprehtárseh oon pokeetoh máss.)

Vous êtes bien trop jeune pour voyager toute seule—vous n'avez même pas seize ans, je parie?

(Voozait byan tro shern poor vwayahshay too serl—voo navay maim par saizan, sher paree?)

Mi sembra troppo giovane per viaggiare da sola—ha compiuto sedici anni?

(Mee sehm-brah trop-poh joh-vah-neh per vee-ah-jah-reh dah soh-lah: ah compee-oo-toh seh-dee-chee ahn-nee?)

Parece muy joven para viajar sola . . ¿Ha cumplido ya dieciséis años?

(Parétheh mooy hóben párah beeyahhár sólah . . . Ah koompleedoh yáh dyéthisséis ányoss?)

15

IN THE TRAIN

Aren't you Miss Bardot?

Sind Sie nicht Fräulein Bardot?

(Zind zi nisht fräulyn Bardot?)

My eyes hurt, may I turn out the light?

Meine Augen vertragen das Licht nicht; darf ich es ausknipsen?

(Myne aogen fertraagen das lisht nisht; daarf ish es aoscknipzen?)

Let me help you with your case.

Erlauben Sie—darf ich mit Ihrem Gepäck helfen?

(Erlaoben zi, daarf ish mit iren gepeck helfen?)

I'm sorry but it's so crowded, I can't move my hands.

Tut mir leid, es ist nicht möglich, meine Hände wegzunehmen in diesem Gedränge.

(Toot mir lyd, es ist nisht moeglish, myne hande vaigtsoonemen in dizem gedraynge.)

Let me stay on the floor of your sleeper—I won't be in the way.

Darf ich nicht in Ihrem Schlafwagen auf dem Fussboden liegen—das stört Sie doch sicherlich nicht.

(Daarf ish nisht in irem schlaaf-vaagen aof dem fossboden ligen—das shtoert zi doch zisherlish nisht.)

FRENCH	ITALIAN	SPANISH

Vous ne seriez pas Brigitte Bardot, par exemple?

(Voon sehryay par Breesheet Bahrdo, pahr exampl?)

Ma lei non è la Bardot?

(Mah leh-ee non eh lah Bardot?)

¿No es usted miss Bardot?

(Noh ess oosté miss Bardot?)

Cette lumière me fatigue un peu les yeux, vous permettez que j'éteigne?

(Set limyair mer fateeg an per laiz yer, voo pairmetay ker shettain?)

Mi bruciano gli occhi—posso spenger la luce?

(Mee broo-chee-ah-noh lee ock-kee—poh-soh spehn-jer lah loo-cheh?)

Me duelen los ojos, ¿puedo apagar la luz?

(Meh dwéllen loss óhhoss, pwéddoh apahgárr lah looth?)

Laissez-moi vous aider à placer votre valise.

(Laissay-mwar voo zaiday ar plahsay votr valeez.)

Permetta che l'aiuti con la valigia.

(Per-met-tah keh lah-yew-tee kohn lah vah-lee-jah.)

Permítame que la ayude con sus paquetes.

(Permeetah-meh ké lah ah-yoodeh kón soos packétess.)

Je m'excuse, mais il y a tellement de monde que je ne peux même pas bouger les mains.

(Sher mexkiz, maizeelyar tellman der mond ker shern per maim par booshay lay man.)

Mi dispiace, ma siamo cosí pigiati che non riesco a muovere le mani.

(Mee deespee-ah-cheh, mah see-ah-moh koh-zy pee-jah-tee keh non ree-eh-skoh ah moo-oh-veh-reh leh mah-nee.)

Lo siento, pero hay tanta gente que no puedo quitar de ahí las manos.

(Loh seeyéntoh, péroh áy tántah hénteh ké nó pwéddoh keetár dé ah-ee lass mánoss.)

Je vais rester par terre dans vǫtre couchette, comme ça je ne vous gênerai pas.

(Sher vay restay pahr terr dan votr cooshet, com sah shern voo shainray par.)

Lasci che mi metta per terra nel suo vagone letto—non le darò nessuna noia.

(Lah-shee keh mee met-tah per ter-rah nehl soo-oh vah-goh-neh let-toh—non leh dah-ròh nes-soo-nah noh-ee-ah.)

Déjame quedar debajo de tu litera. No te molestaré.

(Déhhameh keddár debáhho dé too leetérah. Nó té molesstáréh.)

IN THE STREET

Excuse me is this five-pound note yours?

Verzeihen Sie bitte, gehört der Fünzigmarkschein Ihnen?

(Fertsyn zi bitte, gehurt der fuenftzig-markshyn inen?)

Can you direct me to the lonely hearts club?

Können Sie mir den Weg zum Club Einsamer Herzen zeigen?

(Koennen zi mir dayn vayg tsoom cloob ynzamer hairtsen tsygen?)

I didn't mean to bump into you.

Entschuldigung, das war nicht meine Absicht.

(Endshooldigoong, daas vaar nisht myne upsisht.)

I'm sorry, I mistook you for Elizabeth Taylor.

Verzeihung, ich habe Sie mit Elisabeth Taylor verwechselt.

(Fertsy-oong, ish haabe zi mit Elizabeth Taylor fervayxelt.)

Hello, Beautiful!

Hallo, Prachtstück!

(Hallo, praacht-shtuek.)

FRENCH	ITALIAN	SPANISH
Excusez-moi, il est à vous ce billet de mille?	Scusi, è sua questa banconota?	Perdona, ¿ es tuyo este billete de quinientas pesetas?
(Exkizay-mwar, eel aitar voo ser beeyayd meel?)	*(Skoo-zee eh soo-ah kwestah ban-ko-noh-tah?)*	*(Perdónah, éss tooyoh ésteh billyéteh dé keenyéntass pessétass?)*
Pouvez-vous m'indiquer où se trouve le club des cœurs solitaires?	C'è un locale dove un povero cane solitario può trovare un po' di compagnia?	¿Puedes decirme dónde está el club de los corazones solitarios?
(Poovay-voo mandeekay oo ser troov ler clerb day ker soleetair?)	*(Chèh oon local-eh doh-veh oon poh-veh-roh cah-neh solitar-eeoh pwo troh-vah-reh oon poh dee compah-nee-ah?)*	*(Pwéddes dethirmeh dóndeh stá él cloob dé lóss korathóness solitáryoss?)*
Je n'ai pas fait exprès.	L'assicuro non era mia intenzione urtarla.	No quería darte este empujón.
(Sher nay par fay expray.)	*(Lahs-see-coo-roh non eh-rah mee-ah inten-tzee-oh-neh oor-tar-lah.)*	*(Noh kereeyah dárteh ésteh empoohhón.)*
Je m'excuse, je vous ai prise pour Elizabeth Taylor.	Scusi, l'avevo presa per Elizabeth Taylor.	Lo siento. Te tomé por Elisabeth Taylor.
(Sher mexkiz, sher voozay preez poor Aileezabet Taylohr.)	*(Skoo-zee, lah-veh-voh preh-za per Elizabeth Taylor.)*	*(Loh seeyéntoh. Té tohmé pór Elisabeth Taylor.)*
Bonjour, Beauté!	Ciao, bellezza!	¡Hola, guapa!
(Bonshoor, Bawtay!)	*(Chow bel-lets-ah!)*	*(Olah, gwappah!)*

IN THE STREET

I am a talent scout.

Ich bin auf Talentsuche.
(Ish bin aof talent-zooche.)

I am an artist—will you pose for me?

Ich bin Maler, würden Sie für mich sitzen?
(Ish bin maaler, vuerden zi fuer mish zitsen?)

May I walk with you?

Darf ich Sie begleiten?
(Darf ish zi beglyten?)

You have such an attractive face.

Sie haben ein unerhört reizvolles Gesicht.
(Zi haaben yn oonairhoert rytsfolles gezisht.)

I'm lost; can you help me?

Ich habe mich verlaufen; können Sie mir helfen?
(Ish haabe mish ferlaofen; koennen zi mir haylfen?)

How do I get to ......?

Wie komme ich nach ......?
(Vi komme ish naach ......?)

Je suis à la recherche de talents inconnus. *(Sher sweezar la rehshairsh der talan zanconni.)*	È il mio mestiere scoprire nuove stelle. *(Eh eel mee-oh meh-stee-eh-reh sko-pree-reh noo-oh-veh stehl-leh.)*	Soy un hábil explorador. *(Sóy oon ábeel exploradór.)*
Je suis peintre—voulez-vous poser pour moi? *(Sher swee pantr—voolay-voo pozay poor mwar?)*	Sono un artista; mi fa da modella? *(Soh-noh oon artee-stah: mee fah dah model-lah?)*	Soy pintor . . . ?quieres ser mi modelo? *(Sóy peentór . . . keeyéress sér mee modéloh?)*
Puis-je vous accompagner? *(Pweesh voo zacompanyay?)*	Posso accompagnarla? *(Possoh ak-kompah-nee-ar-lah?)*	¿Quieres que te acompañe? *(Keeyéress ké té akom-pányeh?)*
Votre visage est si adorable! *(Votr veezash ay see ador-ahbl!)*	Ha un volto cosí affa-scinante. *(Ah oon voltoh koh-zée af-fah-shee-nan-teh.)*	¡Tienes un rostro tan atractivo . . .! *(Teeyénness oon rróstroh tán atracteeboh . . .!)*
J'ai perdu mon chemin, voulez-vous m'aider? *(Shay perdi mon sherman, voolay-voo maiday?)*	Ho perso la strada; mi può aiutare? *(Oh per-soh lah strah-dah: mee pwo ah-ee-oo-ta-reh?)*	Me he perdido. ¿Podrías ayudarme? *(Meh eh perdeedoh. Pod-reeyass ahyudármeh?)*
S'il vous plaît, pour aller à . . . . . . ? *(Seel voo play, poor allay ar . . . . . . ?)*	Mi può dire la strada per . . . . . . ? *(Mee pwo dee-reh lah strah-dah per . . . . . . ?)*	¿Cómo podría llegar hasta . . . . . . ? *(Kómoh podreeyah llyégar ástah . . . . . . ?)*

Didn't we meet in Hollywood, during a film I was producing?	Haben wir uns nicht während der Produktion meines Filmes in Hollywood getroffen? *(Haaben vir oons nisht vairend der prodooktion mynes films in Hollywood getroffen?)*
I can't remember where I parked my Rolls-Royce.	Jetzt weiss ich nicht mehr, wo ich meinen Rolls-Royce geparkt habe. *(Yetst vys ish nisht mair, vo ish mynen Rolls-Royce gepaarkt haabe.)*
Please help me, where is the best place for buying diamonds in ......?	Helfen Sie mir bitte; wo kauft man hier die besten Diamanten? *(Helfen zi mir bitte; vo kaoft man hir di besten di-amaanten?)*
Will you show me where I am on this map?	Zeigen Sie mir bitte auf dem Stadtplan, wo ich mich befinde. *(Tsygen zi mir bitte aof dem shtaatplaan, vo ish mish befinde.)*
That's very confusing; couldn't you take me?	Das finde ich nie; können Sie mich nicht begleiten? *(Daas finde ish ni; koennen zi mish nisht beglyten?)*

FRENCH	ITALIAN	SPANISH

Ne vous ai-je pas vue à Hollywood pendant que je tournais un film?

(Ner voo zaish par vi ar Oleewood pandan kersh toornay an feelm?)

Ma non ci siamo incontrati a Hollywood, durante la lavorazione di un mio film?

(Mah non chee see-ah-moh incon-trah-tee ah Hollywood, doo-ran-teh lah lavorah-tzee oh-neh dee oon mee-oh film.)

¿Nos vimos en Hollywood, en la última película que he producido?

(Noss beemoss én Hollywood, én lá oolteemah peleekoolah ké eh prodootheedoh?)

Je ne sais même plus où j'ai laissé ma Rolls-Royce.

(Shern say maim pli oo shay laisay mar Rolls-Royce.)

Non riesco a ricordarmi dove ho posteggiato la mia Rolls-Royce.

(Non rée-eh-skoh ah reecor-dar-mee doh-veh oh pohsteh-jah-toh lah mee-ah Rolls-Royce.)

No puedo recordar dónde he aparcado mi Rolls-Royce.

(Noh pwéddoh rrecordár dóndeh eh ahparkádoh mee Rolls-Royce.)

Aidez-moi je vous prie: pouvez-vous me montrer la bijouterie où l'on trouve les plus beaux diamants?

(Aiday-mwar, sher voo pree: poovay-voo mer montray la beeshootree oo lon troov lay pli baw dyahman?)

Scusi, ma a ...... dove si comprano i piú bei diamanti?

('Skoo-zee, mah ah ...... doh-veh see kom-pranoh ee pew beh-ee dee-ah-mantee?)

Por favor, ¿cuál es el mejor sitio para comprar diamantes en ......?

(Pór fahbór, kwál ess él mehhór seetyoh párah komprár deeyahmántess én ......?)

Pouvez-vous me montrer où nous sommes sur ce plan?

(Poovay-voo mer montray oo noo som sir ser plan?)

Mi può indicare su questa cartina dove mi trovo ora?)

(Mee pwo indicah-reh soo kwestah car-tee-nah doh-ve mee troh-voh oh-rah?)

¿Podrías indicarme dónde estoy, en este mapa?

(Podreeyass eendeekármeh dóndeh stóy, én ésteh mápah?)

C'est vachement compliqué! Pourriez-vous m'accompagner?

(Say vashman compleekay! Pooriay-voo macompanyay?)

Mi pare molto complicato —lei non mi accompagnerebbe?

(Mee pah-reh moltoh complee-cah-toh—leh-ee non mee accompah-nee-eh-rebbeh?)

Es muy complicado, ¿podrías acompañarme?

(Ess mooy kompleekádoh, podreeyass accompanyármeh?)

23

IN THE RESTAURANT

Is this seat taken?

Ist dieser Platz noch frei?

(*Ist diser plaats noch fry?*)

Smart hotels are so public; are there no places to meet the people?

Elegante Hotels sind so unpersönlich; gibt's hier kein Lokal, wo auch der Mann von der Strasse hingeht?

(*Elegante hotels zind zo oonperzoenlish; gibt's hir kyn lokaal, vo aoch der maan fon der shtraase hingayt?*)

I'm not very hungry. Are you?

Ich bin nicht sehr hungrig. Du?

(*Is bin nisht zair hoongrig. Doo?*)

Just one coffee please, waiter, and two straws.

Ober, zwei Strohhalme und einen Kaffee, bitte.

(*Ober, tsvy shtro-haalme oond ynen kaaffe, bitte.*)

Try some peppers/lychees.

Wie wär's mit Paprikaschoten/ chinesischem Kompott?

(*Vi vair's mit paaprikaa-shoten/ shinayzishem kompott?*)

FRENCH	ITALIAN	SPANISH
Cette place est prise? *(Set plahs ay preez?)*	Questo posto è libero? *(Kwestoh poh-stoh eh leeberoh?)*	¿Está ocupada esta silla? *(Stáh okoopádah éstah seellyah?)*
Les hôtels chics sont de véritables moulins! Où est-ce qu'on peut rencontrer des gens intéressants? *(Lay zotel sheek son der vaireetabl moolan! Oo eskon per rancontray day shan anterraisan?)*	Gli alberghi di lusso sono sempre cosí anonimi; non c'è qualche posto caratteristico dove vanno gli abitanti del luogo? *(Lee albehr-ghee dee loos-soh soh-noh sempreh koh-zeè anonimee: non chèh kwalkeh poh-stoh carat-teh-reestee-koh doh-veh van-noh lee ah-bee-tantee dehl looh-goh?)*	En los hoteles elegantes hay demasiado público; ¿no habrá otros lugares más reservados? *(En loss ohtéless ellegántess áy dehmassyádoh poobleekoh; noh abráh otross loogahress máss reserbádos?)*
Je n'ai pas très faim. Et vous? *(Sher nay par tray fam. Ay voo?)*	Io non ho molta fame. E lei? *(Ee-oh non oh mol-tah fah-meh, eh leh-ee?)*	No tengo mucho apetito, ¿y tú? *(Noh téngoh mootchoh appehteetoh, ee too?)*
Garçon! Juste un café et deux pailles! *(Garson! Shistan café ay der paee!)*	Un caffè solo, cameriere, e due cannucce. *(Oon caf-fèh soh-loh, kah-meh-ree-eh-reh, eh doo-eh kan-noo-cheh.)*	Traiga un solo café, camarero, y dos pajas. *(Tráygah oon sóloh kahfé, kahmaréroh, ᵛee dóss páhhass.)*
Prenez un peu de piment (Li-chi) *(Prehnay an perd peeman (lee-chee).)*	Prenda del caviale/dei nidi di rondine. *(Prehn-dah dehl kah-vee-ah-leh/deh-ee needy dee rondee-neh.)*	¿Te gustan los frutos prohibidos? *(Teh goostan loss frootoss proybidoss?)*

IN THE RESTAURANT

Since I spilt it on you at least I must see you home to change.

Ich habe es verschüttet; darf ich Dich wenigstens nach Haus bringen, damit Du Dich umziehen kannst?

(Ish haabe es fershuettet; daarf ish dish vaynigstens naach haos bringen, damit doo dish oomtsin kaanst?)

ON THE BEACH

Keep still; I am a life-saver.

Bitte, nicht rühren—ich bin ein Lebensretter.

(Bitte, nisht rueren—ish bin yn laybensretter.)

I thought you were unconscious so I gave the kiss of life.

Ich dachte, Sie seien ohmächtig, deshalb habe ich Ihnen den Wiederbelebungs-Kuss gegeben.

(Ish dachte, zi zyn ohnmayshtig, deshaalb haabe ish inen dayn viderbelaybungs-kooss gegayben.)

Let me teach you to swim.

Soll ich Sie Schwimmen lehren?

(Zoll ish zi shwimmen layren?)

Comme c'est de ma faute que ça s'est renversé sur vos habits, laissez-moi vous accompagner chez vous pour vous changer.

(Com sayd mar fawt ker sar say ranvairsay sir vo zabee, laissay-mwar voo zacompanyay shay voo poor voo shanshay.)

Il minimo che posso fare, dato che sono stato io a versarglielo addosso, è accompagnarla a casa a cambiarsi.

(Eel minimoh keh possoh fah-reh, dah-toh keh sohnoh stah-toh ee-oh ah versarlee-eh-loh addos-so, eh akkom-pah-nee-ar-lah ah kahsah ah kam-bee-ar-see.)

Ya que te he manchado, al menos te llevaré a casa para que te cambies.

(Yah ké teh eh mantcháddoh, ál ménoss teh llyebahré ah kássah párah ké teh kámbyess.)

Bouge pas; je viens te sauver la vie.

(Boosh par; sher vyan ter sauvay la vee.)

Stia ferma; non vorrei che annegasse.

(Stee-ah fehrma; non vorray keh an-neh-gas-seh.)

Quédate quieta; soy el salvavidas.

(Kédahteh keeyétah; sóy él sahlbábeedass.)

J'ai cru que tu t'es évanouie, alors je t'ai donné le baiser de vie.

(Shay crik tittay zehvahnwee, alohr shtay donnayl baizay der vee.)

Pensavo che avesse perduto i sensi e allora le ho dato il bacio della vita.

(Pen-sah-voh keh avehs-seh per-doo-toh ee sensee eh allorah leh oh datoh eel bacho dehl-la veeta.)

Creí que estabas inconsciente, por esto te hice el boca a boca.

(Kreh-ee ké stábass eenkonsciénteh, pór ésso teh eethe él bókah ah bókah.)

Je vais t'apprendre à nager.

(Sh'vay taprandr ar nashay.)

Le insegno io a nuotare.

(Leh inseh-neeo ee-oh ah noo-oh-tareh.)

¿Quieres que te enseñe a nadar?

(Keeyéress ké teh ensénye ah nahdár?)

Let me shade you with my shoulder.

Schützen Sie sich hinter meinen Schultern gegen die Sonne.

(Shuetsen zi zish hinter mynen shooltern gaygen di zonne.)

Were those men bothering you?

Haben diese Männer Sie belästigt?

(Haaben dise maynner zi belaystigt?)

When does your mother go away?

Wann geht denn Deine Mutter endlich fort?

(Van gayt denn dine mootter ayndlish fort?)

You look cold; let me dry you with this towel.

Sie frieren ja; darf ich Sie abtrocknen?

(Zi friren yaa; darf ish zi abtroknen?)

Let me get the sand off your swimsuit.

Lassen Sie mich den Sand von Ihrem Badeanzug abwischen.

(Lassen zi mish dayn zand fon irem baadeaantsoog abwishen.)

Is this the top of your bikini?

Ist das das Bikini-Oberteil?

(Ist das das bikini obertyl?)

Mets-toi à l'ombre de mon épaule.	Le faccio io ombra con la spalla.	¿Quieres que te haga sombra con mi cuerpo?
(May twar ar lombr d'mon aypawl.)	*(Leh fah-cho ee-oh ombrah con lah spahl-lah.)*	*(Keeyéress ké teh ágah sómbrah kón mee kwérpoh?)*
Ils t'embêtaient ces gars-là?	Quegli uomini le davano fastidio?	¿Te molestaban estos tipos?
(Eel tambaitay say gala?)	*(Kwelly oo-oh-meeny leh dah-vah-noh fastee-deeoh?)*	*(Teh molesstábahn stos teepos?)*
Quand est-ce qu'elle part ta maman?	Quando se ne va sua madre?	¿Cuándo se marcha tu mamá?
(Kanteskel parr ta maman?)	*(Kwando seh neh vah soo-ah mah-dreh?)*	*(Kwándoh sé mártchah too mahmá?)*
On dirait que tu as froid; je vais te sécher avec cette serviette.	Ma lei ha freddo; mi permetta di asciugarla.	Me parece que tienes frío, voy a secarte con la toalla.
(On deerayk tair frwar; sher vay tsaichay aveck set serviette.)	*(Mah leh-ee ah frehd-doh; mee permet-tah dee ashew-garlah.)*	*(Mé pahrétheh ké teeyénnes freeyoh, bóy ah sehkárteh kón lah toahllya.)*
Attends, je vais enlever le sable de ton maillot de bain.	Gliela tolgo io la sabbia dal costume.	Déjame que te quite la arena del bañador.
(Attan, shvay anlervay ler sabl der ton mahyod ban.)	*(Lee-eh-lah tolgoh ee-oh lah sab-beea dal koh-stoo-meh.)*	*(Déhhameh ké té keeteh lá ahrénah dél bahnyádor.)*
C'est le haut de ton bikini, ça?	Questo è parte del suo bikini?	¿Esto es la parte superior del bikini?
(Say ler o der ton bikini, sah?)	*(Kwestoh eh parteh dehl soo-oh bikini?)*	*(Éstoh éss lah párteh sooperiór dél bikíni?)*

29

ON THE BEACH

It's the newest artificial respiration.

Das ist die neueste Wiederbelebungstechnik.

(Das ist di noyste viderbelaybungs-teshnik.)

Have some of my suntan lotion; I'll spread it for you.

Nehmen Sie etwas von meinem Sonnenöl; ich reibe es ein.

(Naymen zi etvas fon mynem zonnenoel; ish rybe es yn.)

I'll hold the towel while you change behind it.

Ich halte das Badetuch und Sie können sich dahinter umziehen.

(Ish halte das badetooch oond zi koennen zish dahinter oomtsin.)

SOME USEFUL WORDS

Couch.

Couch.

(Couch.)

Divan.

Divan.

(Divan.)

Bunk.

Koje

(Koje.)

FRENCH	ITALIAN	SPANISH
Ce que je fais là, c'est la toute dernière méthode de respiration artificielle.	È il metodo piú moderno di respirazione artificiale.	Es un nuevo sistema de respiración artificial.
(Ser ker shfay lar, say la toot dairnyair maitod der raispeerasyon arteefeesiel.)	*(Eh eel metodoh pew modern-oh dee reh-spee-rah-tzee-oh-neh artee-fee-cha-leh.)*	*(Ess oon nwévoh systemah dé respirathión artifithiál.)*
Prends un peu de mon huile de bronzage; attends, je vais te l'étaler moi-même.	Prenda un po' della mia lozione antisolare; gliela spalmo io.	Toma un poco de loción solar; yo mismo te la pondré.
(Pran an pehr d'mon weel der bronzash; attan, shvay ter lettahlay mwar-maim.)	*(Prehn-dah oon poh dehl-la mee-ah loh-tzee-oh-neh anti-soh-la-reh; lee-eh-lah spalmoh ee-oh.)*	*(Tómah oon pókoh dé lohtheeyón solár; yó meesmoh té lá pondréh.)*
Je vais te cacher avec la serviette pendant que tu te changes.	Può cambiarsi dietro l'asciugamano; glielo reggo io.	Te aguantaré la toalla mientras te cambias de ropa.
(Shvay tcashay aveck la serviette pandunk ti ter shansh.)	*(Può cahm-beear-see dee-eh-troh lashew-gah-manoh; lee-eh-lo reh-go ee-oh.)*	*(Té ahgooantahré la tóahllya meeyéntrass té kámbeeyas dé rrópah.)*

Un sofa.	Canapè.	Lecho.
(An sawfah.)	*(Cah-nah-péh.)*	*(Letchoh.)*
Un divan.	Divano.	Diván.
(An deevan.)	*(Dee-vah-no.)*	*(Deebáhn.)*
Une couchette.	Branda.	Litera.
(In cooshett.)	*(Brahn-dah.)*	*(Leetérah.)*

I am a masseur; let me loosen up your muscles.

Ich bin Masseur; soll ich Ihre Muskeln auflockern?

(Ish bin maassoer; zoll ish ire moosceln aoflockern?)

I couldn't help hugging you, I got so excited by the game.

Ich musste Sie in die Arme nehmen, das Spiel hat mich so aufgeregt.

(Ish mooste zi in di arme naymen, das shpil haat mish zo aofgeraygt.)

You'd play better in a shorter skirt.

In einem kürzeren Röckchen würden Sie noch besser spielen.

(In ynem kurtseren roeck-shen vuerden zi noch besser shpilen.)

Let me bandage your knee.

Darf ich Ihr Knie bandagieren?

(Darf ish ir cni baandajiren?)

These crushes in crowds are so friendly.

So ein Gedränge ist so freund-schaftlich.

(Zo yn gedrenge ist zo froynt-shaftlish.)

Je suis masseur de profession, je vais vous détendre les muscles.

(*Sher swee massehr der professyon, sher vay voo daitandr lay miskl.*)

Sono un massaggiatore; lasci che le sciolga i muscoli.

(*Soh-noh oon massah-jahtoh-reh; lashee keh leh shohlgah ee moo-skoh-lee.*)

Soy masajista; déjame que te relaje los músculos.

(*Sóy massahheestah; déhhah-meh ké teh rrehláhheh loss mooskooloss.*)

Je ne peux pas m'empêcher de vous serrer dans mes bras, tellement le jeu me fascine!

(*Shern per par manpaishay der voo serray dan may brah, tellman ler sher mer faseen!*)

È stata l'emozione del gioco —non ho potuto fare a meno di abbracciarla.

(*Eh stah-tah leh-moh-tzeeoneh dehl joh-koh—non oh poh-too-toh fah-reh ah mehnoh dee ab-bra-char-lah.*)

No podría hacer lucha contigo; este juego me pone muy nervioso.

(*Noh podreeyah athér lootchah kón-teegoh; ésteh hooéhgoh meh póneh mooy nerbeeyóssoh.*)

Vous joueriez tellement mieux en jupe courte!

(*Voo shooryay tellman myer an ship coort!*)

Se avesse la gonna piú corta giocherebbe meglio.

(*Seh ah-vehs-seh lah gohnnah pew kor-tah joh-kehreh-beh meh-lee-oh.*)

Jugarías mejor con una faldita más corta.

(*Hoogahreeyass mehhór kón oonah fahldeetah máss kórtah.*)

Je vais vous mettre un bandage autour du genou.

(*Sher vay voo metr an bandash awtoor di shernoo.*)

Le fascio io il ginocchio.

(*Leh fah-shoh ee-oh eel jeenock-keeoh.*)

¿Quieres que te vende la rodilla?

(*Keeyéress ké teh béndeh lah rrohdeellyah?*)

C'est tellement amusant d'être serrés ainsi dans la foule.

(*Say tellman amizan daitr serray ansee dan la fool.*)

Questo pigia pigia tra la folla è cosí piacevole.

(*Kwestoh pee-jah pee-jah' trah lah follah èh ko-zée pee-ah-cheh-voh-leh.*)

Estos apretujones entre la multitud resultan muy amistosos.

(*Estoss ahprehtoo-hóness éntreh lá moolteetooth ressultan mooy ahmeestósoss.*)

SPORTS

Let me teach you judo.

Ich möchte Ihnen so gerne Judo beibringen.

(Ish moeshte inen zo gairn Judo bybringen.)

I'll hold you so you don't fall over.

Kommen Sie, ich halte Sie, damit Sie nicht hinfallen.

(Kommen zi, ish haalte zi, damit zi nisht hinfallen.)

But the man always does that in acrobatic skating.

Das soll aber der Mann beim akrobatischen Eislaufen machen.

(Daas zoll aaber der maann bym akrobaatishen icelaofen maachen.)

IN THE CINEMA

Let's go to a horror film.

Sehen wir uns doch einen Horror-film an.

(Zayn vir oons doch ynen horror-film an.)

No, the back row, please.

Nein, bitte die letzte Reihe.

(Nyn, bitte di laytste ryhe.)

FRENCH	ITALIAN	SPANISH
Je vais vous apprendre le judo. *(Sher vay voo zapprandr ler shido.)*	Le insegno l'arte del judo. *(Le een-seh-nee-oh larteh dehl judoh.)*	¿Quieres que te enseñe judo? *(Keeyéress ké teh ehnsénye hoodoh?)*
Je vous tiendrai, comme ça vous ne tomberez pas. *(Sher voo tyandray, com sah voon tombray par.)*	La reggo, così non cade. *(Lah reh-goh, ko-zée non cah-deh.)*	Te sostendré para que no te caigas. *(Teh sostendréh párah ké noh teh káygass.)*
Mais le cavalier fait toujours ça dans les figures sur glace! *(May ler cavalyay fay tooshoor sah dan lay feegir sir glass!)*	Ma nelle acrobazie sul ghiaccio l'uomo fa sempre così! *(Mah nehl-leh ah-croh-bah-tzee-eh sool ghee-ah-chee-oh loo-oh-moh fah sehm-preh koh-zée.)*	En el patinaje artístico, el hombre siempre lo hace así. *(Én él pateenáhheh artisticoh, él ómbreh seeyémpreh loh átheh assee.)*
Allons voir un film d'épouvante. *(Ahlon vwar an feelm daipoovant.)*	Andiamo a vedere un film dell'orrore. *(An-dee-ah-moh ah veh-deh-reh oon film dehl-or-roh-reh.)*	Vamos a ver una película de miedo. *(Bámos ah bér oonah pehlee-koolah dé meeyédoh.)*
Non, pas ici; la dernière rangée s'il vous plaît. *(Non, pazeecee; la dairnyair ranshay, seel voo play.)*	No, nell'ultima fila per favore. *(Noh, nehl-ool-tee-mah fee-lah per fah-voh-reh.)*	No, la última fila, por favor. *(Noh, lah oolteemah feelah, pórr fahbórr.)*

IN THE CINEMA

I'm terribly sorry, I thought it was the arm-rest.

Tut mir sehr leid, aber ich dachte es sei die Armlehne.

(*Toot mir zehr lyd, aber ish dachte es zy di armlayne.*)

Let me move your coat.

Ich nehme schon ihren Mantel.

(*Ish nayme shon iren mantel.*)

I can't move my knee, these seats are so narrow.

Die Sitze sind zu eng, da kann ich mein Knie nicht wegnehmen.

(*Di zitse zind tsoo ayng, da kan ish myn cni nisht vaygnaymen.*)

I'm sorry my ice-cream has dropped down your dress, let me get it out for you.

O, entschuldigen Sie, jetzt ist mein Eis in Ihre Bluse gefallen. Darf ich es wieder rausnehmen?

(*O, entshooldigen zi, yetst ist myn yce in ire bloose gefallen, darf ish es vider roasnaymen?*)

FRENCH	ITALIAN	SPANISH

Je m'excuse, j'ai cru que c'était l'accoudoir.

(Sher mexkiz, shay cri ker setay lakoodwar.)

Mi scusi tanto, credevo fosse il bracciolo della poltrona.

(Mee scoo-zee tan-toh, crehdeh-voh fos-seh eel brahcho-loh dehl-la pol-trohnah.)

Lo siento mucho, creí que era el brazo de la butaca.

(Loh seeyéntoh mootchoh, kreh-ee ké érah él brátho dé lah boottakah.)

Laissez-moi vous débarrasser de votre manteau.

(Laisay-mwar voo daibarasay der votr manto.)

Posso spostare il suo cappotto?

(Pos-soh spoh-stah-reh eel soo-oh cap-pot-toh?)

Permíteme que te quite la chaqueta.

(Permeeteh-meh ké teh keeteh lah tchakétah.)

Je ne peux même pas bouger les genoux, ces fauteuils sont si étroits!

(Shern per maim par booshay lay shernoo, say fotey son see aitrwar!)

Non riesco a muovere il ginocchio, questi sedili sono cosí stretti.

(Non ree-eh-scoh ah moooh-veh-reh eel gee-nok-keeoh, kwe-stee seh-dee-lee sonoh coh-zeé streht-tee.)

No puedo mover las rodillas, estos asientos son muy estrechos.

(Noh pwéddoh mohbér lass rrohdeellyas, éstos assyéntos són mooy strétchos.)

Je m'excuse, ma glace est tombée dans votre col; je vais l'enlever.

(Sher mexkiz, ma glass ay tombay dan votr col; sher vay lanl'vay.)

Mi dispiace che il mio gelato sia finito nella scollatura del suo abito. Permette che lo riprenda?

(Mee dee-spee-ah-cheh keh eel mee-oh jeh-lah-toh see-ah fee-nee-toh nel-lah skol-latoo-rah dehl soo-oh ah-beetoh. Per-met-teh keh loh reepren-dah?)

Lo siento, se me ha caido el helado sobre tu vestido. Te lo limpiaré.

(Loh seeyéntoh, seh mé ah kah-eedoh él ehládoh sóbreh too behsteedoh. Teh loh leempyaréh.)

IN THE CINEMA

Hold my hand—I'm frightened.

Ich fürchte mich—halten Sie bitte meine Hand.

(Ish fuershte mish—halten zi bitte myne haand.)

I dropped my glove down there.

Ich suche da unten nur meinen Handschuh.

(Ish zooche da oonten noor mynen haandshoo.)

How do these fasteners work?

Wie macht man den Verschluss auf?

(Vi macht maan dayn fershloos oaf?)

AT THE ART GALLERY

Please forgive me but I find Constable uncontrollably sexy.

Sie müssen mir schon verzeihen, aber ich finde Constable hemmungslos sexy.

(Zi muessen mir shon fertsyn, aber ish finde Constable haymmoongslos sexy.)

Are you a model? Starkers?

Sind Sie Aktmodell?

(Zind zi aaktmodell?)

Gardez ma main dans la vôtre, j'ai peur!

(Garday ma man dan la votr, shay pehr!)

Mi tenga la mano, ho paura.

(Mee ten-gah lah mah-noh, oh pah-oo-rah.)

Cógeme la mano . . .Tengo miedo.

(Kóhheh-meh lah mánoh . . . Téngoh meeyéddoh.)

J'ai perdu mon gant là-dessous.

(Shay pairdi mon gan ladsoo.)

Sto cercando il mio guanto.

(Stoh chair-can-doh eel mee-oh gwantoh.)

Se me ha caido un guante ahí debajo.

(Seh mé ah kah-eedoh oon gwánteh ah-ee dehbáhhoh.)

Comment vous les dégrafez vos trucs?

(Comman voo lay daigraffay vo tric?)

Com'è complicata questa chiusura.

(Koh-mèh cohm-plee-kah-tah kwe-stah kew-soo-rah.)

¿Cómo funcionan esos cierres?

(Kómoh foontheeyónan éssos thiérres?)

Je vous prie de m'excuser, mais je trouve les tableaux de Constable terriblement sexy.

(Sher voo pree de mexkizay, may sher troov lay tablaw de Constable terreeblman sexy.)

Mi perdoni, ma questo artista lo trovo veramente perturbante.

(Mee pehr-dohnee, mah kwehsto artist-ah lo trovo veh-rah-mehnteh per-toor-bahnteh.)

Discúlpame, por favor, pero a Constable lo encuentro descaradamente sexual.

(Disskoolpah-meh, pórr fahbórr, péroh ah Constáhbbleh loh enkwéntroh desskahrádaménteh sekswál.)

Vous êtes modèle? Vous faites du nu?

(Voot zait modell? Voo fait di ni?)

Posa da modella? Nuda?

(Pohsah dah model-lah? Noo-dah?)

¿Eres modelo? ¿ De desnudos?

(Éress mohdéloh? Deh dessnoodoss?)

AT THE ART GALLERY

Please don't move; you look more beautiful than all these pictures.

Bleiben Sir doch bitte 'mal still stehen; Sie sind ja viel schöner als alle Gemälde hier.

(Blyben zi doch bitte 'maal shtill shtehn; zi zind yaa fiel shoener als alle modelle hier.)

IN YOUR FLAT

I'm sorry you can't meet them— my parents have been suddenly called away for the weekend.

Schade, dass Du meine Eltern nicht treffen kannst. Sie sind plötzlich zum Wochenende fortgefahren.

(Shaade, daass doo myne eltern nisht treffen kaannst. Zi zind ploetslish tsoon vochenende fortgefaaren.)

The etchings are away being framed.

Willst Du wirklich Kaffee trinken?

(Villst doo virklish kaffee trinken?)

It's very lonely here.

Hier ist es sehr einsam.

(Hir ist es zehr ynzam.)

Surtout ne bougez pas, vous êtes tellement plus belle que toutes ces peintures!

(Sirtoo ner booshay par, voo zait tellman pli bell ker toot say pantir.)

La prego, stia ferma. E' piú bella di tutti questi quadri.

(Lah prego, stee-ah fehrmah. Eh pew beh-lah dee tootee kwestee kwah-dree.)

No te muevas, por favor. Eres más hermosa que todos estos cuadros.

(Noh teh mwébass, pórr fahbórr. Éress máss ehrmóssah ké tóddoss éstoss kwádross.)

Je regrette que vous ne puissiez pas voir mes parents, ils sont partis brusquement pour le weekend.

(Sher rergret ker voon pweesyay par vwar may paran, eel son partee briskerman poor ler week-end.)

Mi dispiace di non poterti presentare i miei genitori—sono dovuti andar via all'improvviso per il weekend.

(Mee dees-pee-ah-che dee non po-ter-tee presentah-reh ee mee-eh-ee jeh-nee-tory: soh-noh doh-voo-ty andar vee-ah ahl-limproh-vee-soh per eel weekend.)

Siento que no puedas conocerlos . . . Mis padres han tenido que salir urgentemente de viaje.

(Seeyéntoh ké noh pwéddass konothérloss . . . Miss páddres án tehneedoh ké sahleer oorhénteménteh dé beeyáhhe.)

J'ai donné mes estampes à encadrer.

(Shay donnay may zestamp ar ancadray.)

I quadri che volevo mostrarti sono ancora dal corniciaio.

(Ee kwa-dree keh voleh-voh moh-strar-tee soh-noh ankoh-rah dahl kornee-cha-ee-oh.)

He llevado todos los cuadros a enmarcar.

(Eh llyébádoh tóddos loss kwáddros ah enmaarkár.)

On est très isolé ici.

(Onay tray zeezolay eecee.)

Ci si sente molto soli qui.

(Chee see sehn-teh mohl-toh soh-lee kwee.)

Se está muy solo aquí.

(Sé stá mooy sóloh akee.)

IN YOUR FLAT

I write music/poetry to cover my loneliness.

Ich dichte/komponiere, um die Einsamkeit zu verjagen.

(Ish dishte/komponire, oom di ynzamkyt tsoo feryaagen.)

Let me take your coat.

Komm, gib' mir Deinen Mantel.

(Komm gib' mir dynen maantel.)

Is that embroidery on your blouse?

Ist das Stickerei da an Deiner Bluse?

(Ist daas shtikery daa an dyner bloose?)

Take your shoes off; you'll be more comfortable.

Zieh' Deine Schuhe aus, das ist viel bequemer.

(Tsi dyne shoo aos, daas ist fil bequemer.)

Try a mixed drink instead.

Nimm doch lieber einen Cocktail.

(Nimm doch liber ynen cocktail.)

FRENCH	ITALIAN	SPANISH

Je fais de la musique (j'écris des poèmes) pour oublier ma solitude.

(Sher' fay dlar mizeek (shaykree day po-aim) poor oobleeay ma soleetid.)

Per riempire la mia solitudine scrivo musica/poesia.

(Per ree-ehm-pee-reh lah mee-ah solitoo-dee-neh skree-voh moo-see-kah/ poh-eh-zee-ah.)

Escribo música/poesías para distraer mi soledad.

(Screeboh moosicah/poesíass párah distraér mee soledád.)

Laissez-moi vous débarrasser de votre manteau.

(Laissay-mwar voo daibarassay der votr manto.)

Si vuol togliere il cappotto?

(See voo-ohl toh-lee-eh-reh eel kap-pot-toh?)

Deja que te quite la chaqueta.

(Déhha ké té keeteh lá tchakétah.)

C'est de la broderie ce que vous avez là sur votre chemisier?

(Say dlar brodree ser ker voo zavay lar sir votr shemeezyay?)

Quelli lí sono ricami sulla sua camicetta?

(Kwel-lée-lee soh-noh reekah-mee sool-lah soo-ah kamee-chet-tah?)

¿Este bordado es de tu blusa?

(Esteh bordádoh ess dé too bloosah?)

Débarrassez-vous de vos chaussures, vous serez plus à l'aise!

(Daibarassay-vood vo shawssir, voo sray plizalaiz!)

Si tolga le scarpe; starà piú comoda.

(See tohl-gah leh scar-peh; stah-rah pew ko-moh-dah.)

Quítate los zapatos, estarás más cómoda.

(Kíttateh loss thahpátoss, staráss máss kómohdah.)

Essayez plutôt un cocktail.

(Essaiyay plito an cocktail.)

Provi un po' questo cocktail che ho inventato io.

(Proh-vee oon poh kwestoh cocktail keh oh inven-tahtoh ee-oh.)

Será mejor que tomes un combinado.

(Seráh mehhór ké tómess oon kombeenádoh.)

IN YOUR FLAT

I like the heat full on but take your cardigan/sweater off if it's too hot.

Ich habe die Heizung gern auf Volldampf, zieh' Deinen Pully/Deine Strickjacke aus, wenn's Dir zu warm ist.

(Ish habe di hytsoong gern aof folldaamf; tsi dynen pully/dyne shtrikyacke aos, ven's dir tsoo vaarm ist.)

I haven't a cocktail shaker; this is excitement.

Ich mixe nicht—das ist Aufregung.

(Ish mixe nisht—daas ist aofraygoong.)

Come and see the view from this window by the bed.

Die schönste Aussicht hat man von dem Fenster hier am Bett.

(Di shoenst aosisht hat maan fon dem fenster hir aam bett.)

I can't cook; I live on sandwiches.

Kochen kann ich nicht; ich esse immer nur Schnitten.

(Kochen kaann ish nisht; ish aysse imer noor shnitten.)

FRENCH	ITALIAN	SPANISH
J'aime bien que le chauffage soit à fond, mais si vous avez trop chaud n'hésitez pas à tomber le cardigan (le pull).	A me piace la casa ben riscaldata ma se lei ha troppo caldo si tolga pure il golf.	Me gusta la calefacción a toda marcha, pero puedes quitarte la chaqueta/el jersey, si tienes calor.
(Shaim byan kler shawfash swatar fon, may see voo zavay tro shaw naizeetay pazar tombay ler cardeegan (ler pil).)	*(Ah meh pee-ah-che lah ka-zah ben rees-kal-dah-tah mah seh leh-ee ah trop-poh kal-doh see tohl-gah poo-reh eel golf.)*	*(Meh goostah lá calefakthión ah tóddah márchah, péroh pwéddes kittárteh lá tchakétah/él herséy, see teeyénnes kahlór.)*
Je n'ai pas de shaker; mais je garantis le mélange!	No, non sto agitando il cocktail; sono semplicemente eccitato.	No tengo coctelera; resulta muy excitante.
(Sher nay pard shaikair; may sher garanteel mailansh!)	*(Noh, non stoh ah-jee-tan-doh eel cocktail; soh-noh sehm-plee-che-men-teh etch-chee-tah-toh.)*	*(Noh téngoh cocktelérah; resultah mooy exceetánteh.)*
Viens voir la belle vue qu'on a du lit à travers la fenêtre.	Venga a vedere il panorama da questa finestra vicino al letto.	Ven a mirar el paisaje desde esta ventana junto a la cama.
(Vyan vwahr la bell vi konar di lee a travair la fernaitr.)	*(Vengah ah veh-deh-reh eel panorama dah kwestah fee-neh-strah vee-chee-noh ahl let-toh.)*	*(Bén ah meerár él payssáhhe désdeh éstah bentánah huntoh ah lá kámah.)*
Je ne sais pas faire la cuisine; je me nourris de sandwiches.	Io non so cucinare; vivo di panini.	No sé cocinar; vivo de bocadillos.
(Shern say par fair la cweezeen; sherm nooree de sandweech.)	*(Ee-oh non soh coo-chee-nareh; vee-voh dee pah-nee-nee.)*	*(Noh sé cotheenár; beeboh dé bokadeellyoss.)*

IN YOUR FLAT

I can't operate the cooker.

Keine Ahnung, wie der Kochherd funktioniert.

(*Kyne aanoong, vi der koch-hayrd foonktionirt.*)

I didn't think you'd notice that my things all need mending.

Ist Dir aufgefallen, dass meine Sachen alle repariert werden müssen?

(*Ist dir aofgefallen, daas myne sachen aalle reparirt verden muesse?*)

The buttons and cotton are on that box but I don't know how to use them.

Knöpfe und Garn sind da im Kasten, aber ich kann ja nicht nähen.

(*Knoepfe oond gaarn zind daa im kaasten, aber ish kaan yaa nisht nayen.*)

The fuse has blown.

Jetzt ist Kurzschluss.

(*Yetst ist courts-shlooss.*)

Try dancing in the bedroom, where I keep the radio.

Tanzen wir doch im Schlafzimmer, da ist das Radio.

(*Tantsen vir doch im shlaaftsimmer, daa ist daas raadio.*)

Je ne sais pas faire marcher la cuisinière.

(Shern say par fair marshay la cweezeenyair.)

Non so far funzionare il fornello.

(Non soh far foon-tzee-onah-reh eel for-nehl-loh.)

No sé como funciona la cocina.

(Noh sé kómoh foonthiónah lá kotheenah.)

Je ne pensais pas que vous alliez remarquer que presque tous mes vêtements ont besoin d'être recousus.

(Shern pansay par ker voo zaliay rehmarkay ker presk too may vetman on berzwan daitr rehcoozi.)

Non pensavo ti saresti accorta che tutte le mie cose han bisogno di esser rammendate.

(Non pen-sah-voh tee sareh-stee ak-kor-tah keh toot-teh leh mee-eh ko-seh ahn bee-zoh-neeoh dee esser rah-men-dah-teh.)

No sé si te habrás dado cuenta de que toda mi ropa necesita un buen repaso.

(Noh sé see té abráss dádoh kwéntah dé ké tóddah mee rrópah necessitah oon bwén rrepásoh.)

Le fil et les boutons sont dans cette boîte mais je ne sais même pas comment les prendre.

(Ler feel ay lay booton son dan set bwat may shern say maim par comman lay prandr.)

Filo e bottoni sono su quella scatola, ma io non me ne intendo.

(Fee-loh eh bot-tony soh-noh soo kwel-lah skah-toh-lah, mah ec-oh non meh neh inten-doh.)

Los botones y el hilo están en esta caja, pero no sé como se usan.

(Loss bottóness ee él eeloh stán én éstah cáhhah, péroh nó sé kómoh sé oosan.)

Les plombs ont sauté.

(Lay plon on sautay.)

È saltata una valvola.

(Eh sal-tah-tah oo-nah val-voh-lah.)

Se han fundido los plomos.

(Sé án foondíddoh loss plómoss.)

Viens danser dans ma chambre, c'est là que je mets la radio.

(Vayn dansay dan ma shambr, say lark sher may lar rahdio.)

Vieni a ballare in camera da letto, dove ho la radio.

(Vee-eh-ny ah bal-lah-reh een camerah dah let-toh, do-veh oh lah rah-deeoh.)

Vamos a bailar al dormitorio, donde tengo la radio.

(Bámoss ah baylár ál dor-meettórioh, dóndeh téngoh lá rádioh.)

47

IN YOUR FLAT

I'm sorry the door lock has jammed.	Tut mir leid, das Türschloss klemmt. *(Toot mir lyd, daas tuershloss klemmt.)*
I didn't realise the clock had stopped.	Hab' gar nicht bemerkt, dass die Uhr stehengeblieben ist. *(Haab' gar nisht bemayrkt, daass di oor shtehen gebliben ist.)*
The taxis stopped running an hour ago.	Taxis fahren schon seit einer Stunde nicht mehr. *(Taxis faaren shon zyt yner shtoonde nisht mair.)*
Nobody will know.	Merkt doch kein Mensch. *(Mairkt doch kyn mensh.)*
Why not take a bath? I won't look.	Willst Du nicht baden? Ich gucke nicht. *(Villst doo nisht baaden? Ish gooke nisht.)*
I'm afraid the bathroom door won't shut.	Die Badezimmertür schliesst leider nicht. *(Di baadetsimmer-tuer shlihst lyder nisht.)*

FRENCH	ITALIAN	SPANISH
Zut alors! le verrou est coincé!	Mi spiace, ma si è bloccata la serratura.	Lo siento, la cerradura se ha atascado.
(Zit alor! ler vairoo ay kwansay!)	*(Mee spee-ah-che, mah see eh block-kah-tah lah seh-rah-too-rah.)*	*(Loh seeyéntoh, lah thérrah-doorah sé ah atasskádoh.)*
Je ne me suis même pas aperçu que le réveil s'est arrêté.	Non mi ero accorto che s'era fermato l'orologio.	No me había dado cuenta de que el reloj estaba parado.
(Shern mer swee maim par zapairsi kerl raivay set arettay.)	*(Non mee eh-roh ak-kor-toh keh seh-rah fer-mah-toh loh-roh-loh-jee-oh.)*	*(Noh mé abbíah dádoh kwéntah dé ké él rrelóhh stábah pahrádoh.)*
Ça fait une heure que les taxis ont cessé de circuler.	Non ci sono piú tassí a quest'ora.	Los taxis ya no circulan desde hace una hora.
(Sar fay in ehr ker lay taxee on cessay dseerkilay.)	*(Non chee soh-noh pew tas-sée ah kwestoh-rah.)*	*(Loss táxis yah nó thirkoolan désdeh átheh oonah órah.)*
Personne ne le saura.	Non lo saprà nessuno.	Nadie lo sabrá.
(Pairsonn ner ler sawrah.)	*(Non loh sah-pràh nes-soo-noh.)*	*(Náddye loh sabráh.)*
Tu peux prendre un bain, tu sais . . . Je ne regarderai pas!	Fa un bagno. Io non guardo.	¿Por qué no te bañas? No miraré.
(Ti per prandr an ban, ti say . . . Shern rehgardray par!)	*(Fah oon bah-nee-oh. Ee-oh non goo-ar-doh.)*	*(Pór ké nó teh bányass? Nó meerah-rěh.)*
J'ai bien peur qu'on ne puisse pas fermer à clé la porte de la salle de bain.	Mi dispiace, ma la porta del bagno non si chiude.	Lamento mucho que la puerta del baño no cierre.
(Shay byan pehr koon pwees par fairmay ar clay la port der la sal der ban.)	*(Mee deespee-ah-cheh, mah lah portah dehl bah-nee-oh non see kew-deh.)*	*(Laméntoh mootchoh ké lá pwértah dél bányo nó theey-érreh.)*

IN HER FLAT

Its rather warm, may I take my jacket off?

Es ist recht warm hier, darf ich meine Jacke ausziehen?

(Es ist raycht vaarm hir, daarf ish myne yaacke oastsihen?)

I bought a bottle of something unusual for a change.

Ich habe heute zur Abwechslung ein ganz besonderes Fläschchen gekauft.

(Ish haabe hoyte tsoor abvayxloong yn gaans bezondres flaysh-shen gekaoft.)

Where is the bedroom?

Wo ist das Schlafzimmer?

(Vo ist daas schlaaftsimmer?)

I'm tired, may I lie down?

Ich bin müde—darf ich mich ein Weilchen hinlegen?

(Ish bin muede—darf ish mish yn vylshen hinlaygen?)

Why don't you lie down as well? You look a bit tired.

Leg' Dich doch auch ein Weilchen hin, Du siehst auch müde aus.

(Layg' dish doch aoch yn vylshen hin, doo zïst aoch muede aos.)

FRENCH	ITALIAN	SPANISH

Il fait un peu chaud; vous permettez que je tombe la veste?

(Eel faitan per shaw; voo pairmetay ker sher tomb la vest?)

Fa piuttosto caldo, posso togliermi la giacca?

(Fah pewt-toh-stoh kal-doh, pos-soh toh-lee-ehr-mee lah jah-kah?)

Hace calor, ¿ puedo quitarme la americana?

(Athe kahlór, pwéddo kittármeh lá americánah?)

J'ai apporté une petite bouteille qui est pas piquée des hannetons.

(Shay apportay in pteet bootay kee nay par peekay day anton.)

Tanto per cambiare ho comprato una bottiglia di qualcosa di insolito.

(Tahn-toh per cahm-bee-ah-reh oh kom-prah-toh oonah bot-tee-lee-ah dee kwal-ko-sah dee een-soh-lee-toh.)

Compré una botella de algo raro, para variar.

(Kompré oonah bottehllya dé álgoh rároh, párah baree-yár.)

Où est la chambre à coucher?

(Oo ay la shambr ar cooshay?)

Dov'è la camera da letto?

(Doh-vèh lah camerah dah let-toh?)

¿Dónde está el dormitorio?

(Dóndeh stá él dormeet-tórioh?)

Je me sens un peu fatigué; est-ce que je peux m'étendre un moment?

(Sherm san an per fateegay; esker sher per maitandr an moman?)

Sono stanco, posso sdraiarmi?

(Soh-no stahn-koh, pos-soh sdrah-eearmee?)

Estoy cansado, ¿puedo estirarme un rato?

(Stóy kansádoh, pwéddoh steerármeh oon rátoh?)

Viens un peu près de moi! Tu as l'air fatiguée.

(Vyan an per pray der mwar! Ti ar lair fateegay.)

Perché non ti sdrai anche tu? Mi sembri un po' stanca.

(Per-kéh non tee sdrah-ee an-keh too? Mee sehm-bree oon poh stahn-kah.)

¿Por qué no te acuestas tu también? Pareces un poco cansada.

(Pór ké noh té akwéstass too tambeeyén? Paréthess oon pókoh cansádah.)

51

There's a lovely view from this couch.	Schöne Aussicht hat man von hier. *(Shoene aosisht hat maan for hir.)*
I feel faint.	Jetzt werde ich ohnmächtig. *(Jaytst verde ish ohnmayshtig.)*
What lovely smooth hands you have, put them here.	Was für schöne weiche Hände Du hast; leg' sie hier hin. *(Vaas fuer shoene vyshe haynde doo hast; layg zi hir hin.)*
I feel unworthy of anyone as lovely as you are.	So etwas Süsses wie Du bist habe ich nicht verdient. *(Zo etvas zuesses vi doo bist haabe ish nisht ferdihnt.)*
What time does your husband return?	Wann kommt Dein Mann nach Hause? *(Van kommt dyn mann nach haose?)*
I'm here to read the electricity meters.	Ich habe nur die elektrische Zähluhr abgelesen. *(Ish haabe noor di elektrishe tsayloor abgelayzen.)*

FRENCH	ITALIAN	SPANISH
On a une de ces vues, de ce sofa!	C'è una vista stupenda da questo divano.	Se ve una vista preciosa desde esta cama.
(Onar in der say vi, der ser sofar.)	*(Cheh oo-nah vee-stah stoopen-dah dah kwestoh dee-vah-noh.)*	*Sé bé oonah beestah pre-theeósah désdeh éstah kámah.)*
Je me sens mal.	Mi sento svenire.	Me siento desfallecido.
(Sherm san mal.)	*(Mee sen-toh sveh-nee-reh.)*	*(Mé seeyéntoh desfahlly-ethído.)*
Ce que tu as de belles mains…! mets-les là!	Che belle manine morbide, mettile qui.	¡Qué manos tan suaves tienes! ¡Pónlas ahí!
(Sker ti ar der bell man…! may-lay lar!)	*(Keh bel-leh mah-nee-neh mor-bee-deh, met-tee-leh kwee.)*	*(Ke mánoss tán swábes teeyénnes! Pónlass ah-ee.)*
Je me sens indigne d'une belle fille comme toi (vous)	Non sono degno di una deliziosa creatura come te.	Me siento indigno de una mujer tan encantadora como tú.
(Sherm san andeen din bell feey com twar (voo).)	*(Non soh-noh deh-neeo dee oo-nah deh-lee-tzee-oh-zah creh-ah-too-rah koh-meh teh.)*	*(Meh seeyéntoh indígnoh deh oonah moohhér tán enkantahdórah kómoh too.)*
Quand est-ce qu'il rentre, ton mari?	A che ora torna tuo marito?	¿A qué hora vuelve tu marido?
(Kanteskeel rantr, ton maree?)	*(Ah keh oh-rah tor-nah toooh mah-ree-toh?)*	*(Ah ké órah bwélbe too mahríddoh?)*
Je suis venu relever le compteur électrique.	Sono venuto a leggere il contatore dell'elettricità.	He venido a leer el contador de la electricidad.
(Sher swee verni rehlvay ler contehr ellektreek.)	*(Soh-noh veh-noo-toh ah ledge-eh-reh eel kon-tah-toh-reh dehl eh-leh-tree-chee-tàh.)*	*(Eh behneedoh ah leh-ér él kontahdór dé lá electrithi-dád.)*

JAMMED IN THE LIFT (ELEVATOR)

The alarm bell doesn't work.

Der Alarm funktioniert nicht.

(Der alaarm fooktionirt nisht.)

We shall probably be here for hours.

Wir werden hier wohl stundenlang festsitzen.

(Vir verden hir vohl shtoonden-laang festzitsen.)

I know a little game to pass the time.

Sollen wir uns mit einem kleinen Spiel die Zeit vertreiben?

(Zollen vir oons mit ynem klynen shpil di tsit fertryben?)

Lean on me if you like.

Lehnen Sie sich an mich.

(Laynen zi zish aan mish.)

FRENCH	ITALIAN	SPANISH
La sonnette d'alarme ne marche pas. *(La saunet dalarm ner marsh par.)*	Il campanello d'allarme non funziona. *(Eel kahm - pah - nehl - loh dahl-lar-meh non foon-tzee-oh-nah.)*	El timbre de alarma no funciona. *(El teembreh dé ahlármah noh foonthiyónah.)*
On va être coincés ici pendant des heures. *(On va aitr kwansay eecee pandan day zehr.)*	Probabilmente resteremo qui per delle ore. *(Probah-beel-mehn-teh rest-eh-reh-moh kwee per dehl-leh oh-reh.)*	Seguramente pasaremos aquí varias horas. *(Sehgoorahménteh pahsarémos ahkee báreeyas óras.)*
Je connais un petit jeu pour passer le temps. *(Sher connay an ptee sher poor passayl tan.)*	So un bel giuoco per passare il tempo. *(Soh oon behl joh-koh per pass-ah-reh eel tempoh.)*	Conozco un lindo juego para pasar el rato. *(Kohnóthkoh oon leendoh hooégho párah passár él rrátoh.)*
Appuie-toi sur moi, si tu veux. *(Apwee-twar sir mwar, see ti ver.)*	Si appoggi pure a me. *(See ahp-poh-jee poo-reh ah meh.)*	Apóyate en mí, si quieres. *(Appóyahteh én mee, see keeyéress.)*

IN THE HOTEL

Mr. and Mrs. Smith.

Herr und Frau Schmidt.
(Herr oond frao shmitt.)

A room with a double bed.

Bitte ein Zimmer mit Doppelbett.
(Bitte, yn tsimmer mit doppel-bett.)

One lump or two, dear?

Nimmst Du ein oder zwei Stück-chen Zucker?

(Nimmst doo yn oder tsy shtueck-shen tsoocker?)

Of course we are married!

Natürlich sind wir verheiratet!
(Natuerlish zind vir ferhyraatet!)

How dare you!

Was fällt Ihnen ein!
(Vaas faylt ihnen yn?)

But I thought they were real ones.

Ich dachte, die sind echt.
(Ish daachte, di zind aysht.)

FRENCH	ITALIAN	SPANISH

Monsieur et Madame Smith.

(Mersyer ay Madahm Smith.)

Il signore e la signora Smith.

(Eel see-nyo-reh eh lah see-nyo-rah Smith.)

El señor y la señora Smith.

(El sehnyórr ee lah sehn-yórah Smith.)

Une chambre avec un lit à deux places.

(In shambr aveck an lee ar der plahs.)

Una camera matrimoniale.

(Oona camera mah-tree-mo-nee-aleh.)

Una habitación con cama de matrimonio.

(Oonah abeetahthión kón kámah deh matrimónioh.)

Un ou deux morceaux, mon chou?

(Anoo der morsaw, mon shoo?)

Una o due zollette, cara?

(Oona oh dweh tzoh-leh-teh, cah-rah?)

¿Un terrón o dos, querida?

(Oon tehrrón oh dóss, keh-reedah?)

Quelle question! Bien sûr que nous sommes mariés!

(Kel kestyon!) Byan sir ker noo somm mariay!)

Certo che siamo sposati!

(Chair-to keh sya-moh spoh-sahtee!)

¡Claro que estamos casados!

(Clároh ké stámmoss kahs-sádoss!)

Quelle insolence!

(Kel ansolans!)

Come osa?

(Koh-meh oh-sah?)

¿Cómo se atreve?

(Kómoh seh ahtrébeh?)

Et moi qui croyais qu'ils étaient vrais!

(Ay mwar kee crwahyay keel zettay vray!)

Ma io credevo che fossero veri.

(Mah yo creh-deh-vo keh foh-seh-ro veh-ree.)

¡Creí que eran de verdad!

(Kreh-ee ké érahn deh behr-dád.)

IN THE HOTEL

Do you snore?	Schnarchst Du? *(Shnarsh-st doo?)*
Fantastic!	Toll! *(Toll!)*
You'll spoil the creases.	Gib' auf meine Bügelfalten acht. *(Gib' aof myne buegelfaalten aacht.)*
What cold feet you have.	Du hast ja so kalte Füsse. *(Doo hast yaa zo kaalte fuesse.)*
That tickles.	Das kitzelt. *(Das kitselt.)*
How did it get like that?	Wie kommt das? *(Vi kommt das?)*
Undo this, please.	Mach' das bitte 'mal auf. *(Maach das bitte 'maal aof.)*
It's stuck fast.	Es geht nicht auf. *(Es gayt nisht aof.)*

FRENCH	ITALIAN	SPANISH
Tu ronfles? *(Ti ronfl?)*	Tu russi? *(Too roo-ssee?)*	¿Roncas? *(Rónkass?)*
Fantastique! *(Fantasteek!)*	Fantastico! *(Fantastic-o!)*	¡Fantástico! *(Fantásticoh!)*
Tu vas m'esquinter le pli. *(Ti var meskantay ler plee.)*	Sciuperai la piega. *(Shoo-per-ah-ee lah pee-eh-gah.)*	Estropearás los pliegues. *(Strohpeh-ahráss loss pleeyeghess.)*
Oh, ce que tu as les pieds glacés! *(Oh, sker ti ar lay pyay glahsay!)*	Che piedi freddi hai! *(Keh pee-eh-dee freh-dee ah-ee!)*	¡Qué pies tan fríos tienes! *(Ké peeyéss tán freeyoss teeyénness!)*
Ça chatouille. *(Sah shatooy.)*	Mi fa il solletico. *(Mee fah eel sol-leh-tee-ko.)*	Hace cosquillas. *(Átheh koskeellyass.)*
Comment ça se fait? *(Comman sass fay?)*	Come hai fatto? *(Coh-meh ah-ee fah-toh?)*	¿Cómo me he puesto así? *(Kómoh meh eh pwéstoh assee?)*
Défais ca, tu veux? *(Deffay sah, ti ver?)*	Aprimi questo, per favore. *(Ah-pree-mee kweh-sto per fah-voreh.)*	Quítate eso, ¿quieres? *(Kittah-teh éssoh, keeyéress?)*
C'est coincé! *(Say kwansay!)*	Non si apre. *(Non see ah-preh.)*	Está muy apretado. *(Stáh mooy ahprehtádoh.)*

I don't think he believes us.

Dieser Kerl glaubt uns doch nicht.

(Dizer kairl glaobt oons doch nisht.)

Try to look natural.

Benimm Dich ganz natürlich.

(Benimm dish gaans naatuerlish.)

Not so near the window.

Nicht so nah am Fenster.

(Nisht zo naa aam fenster.)

Look the other way; I'm shy.

Dreh' Dich um; ich geniere mich.

(Dray dish oom; ish jeniere mish.)

Hurry up, it's very late.

Beeile Dich, es ist schon sehr spät.

(Be-yle dish, es ist shon zehr shpayt.)

You don't look so heavy.

Du bist gar nicht so dick.

(Doo bist gaar nisht zo dick.)

Do this up, please.

Mach' das bitte 'mal zu.

(Maach' das bitte 'maal tsoo.)

FRENCH	ITALIAN	SPANISH
Je ne crois pas qu'il nous ait crus.	Penso che non ci creda.	Supongo que no nos han creido.
(Shern crwah par keel noo zay cri.)	*(Pen-soh keh non chee creh-dah.)*	*(Sooppóngoh ké noh noss ahn kreh-eedoh.)*
Prends un air naturel.	Cerca di essere naturale.	Trata de aparecer natural.
(Pran anair natirell.)	*(Chair-kah dee eh-seh-reh nah-too-rahleh.)*	*(Trátah deh ahpahrehtherr natoorál.)*
Ne t'approche pas trop de la fenêtre!	Non cosí vicino alla finestra.	No tan cerca de la ventana.
(Ner taprosh par tro der la fernaitr.)	*(Non ko-seé vee-chee-no al-lah fee-nest-rah.)*	*(Noh tán zehrkah deh lah behntánah.)*
Tourne-toi, tu m'intimides.	Guarda dall'altra parte; sono timido.	Mira hacia otra parte; tengo vergüenza.
(Toorn-twar, ti mantee-meed.)	*(Gwar-dah dahl ahl-trah part-eh, sono timid-oh.)*	*(Meerah áthiyah ótrah pár-teh; téngoh behrg-wénthah.)*
Fais vite, il est vachement tard!	Spicciati, è molto tardi.	Date prisa, es muy tarde.
(Fay veet, eel ay vashman tahr!)	*(Spee-chah-tee, eh molto tahr-dee.)*	*(Dáteh preesah, ess mooy tárdeh.)*
T'es pas si lourde que ça.	Non sembreresti tanto pesante.	No parece que peses tanto.
(Tay par see loord ker sah.)	*(Non sehm - breh - rehstee tahn-to peh-sahn-teh.)*	*(Noh parétheh ké pehssess tántoh.)*
Ferme-moi ça s'il te plaît.	Ti dispiace allacciarmi.	¿Quieres abrocharme esto?
(Fairm-mwar sah, seel ter play.)	*(Tee dis-pee-a-cheh allah-char-mee?)*	*(Keeyéress ahbrotchármeh esstoh.)*

Is this the first time?

Das erstemal?
(Das airstemaal?)

Why not?

Warum nicht?
(Varoom nisht?)

It'll be all right, I had mumps last year.

Das macht nichts; ich hatte voriges Jahr Ziegenpeter.

(Das maacht nishts; ish hatte foriges Jaar tsigenpeter.)

I've a book which tells you different ways; the pages are marked.

Ich habe hier ein Buch mit verschiedenen Tips. Die Seiten sind markiert.

(Ish haabe hier yn booch mit fershidenen tips; di zyten zind markiert.)

You wrote it?

Hast Du es geschrieben?
(Hast doo es geshriben?)

C'est la première fois…?	É la prima volta?	¿Es la primera vez?
(Say la prermyair fwar…?)	*(Eh lah pree-mah volt-ah?)*	*(Ess lah preeméhrah béth?)*

Pourquoi pas?	Perché no?	¿Por qué no?
(Poorkwar par?)	*(Per-keh no?)*	*(Pór ké noh?)*

Y a pas de danger, j'ai eu les oreillons l'année dernière!	Non aver paura—ho avuto gli orecchioni l'anno scorso.	Todo irá bien. Tuve las paperas el año pasado.
(Yah pard danshay, shay i lay zorayon lannay dernyair!)	*(Non ah-vehr pah-oo-ra, oh ah-vooto lee oh-reh-kioh-nee l'ahno scor-so.)*	*(Tóddoh eeráh beeyén. Toobeh lass pahpérass él ányoh passádoh.)*

J'ai un livre qui indique toutes les positions; jette un coup d'œil, j'ai marqué les pages.	Ho un manuale che insegna metodi diversi: le pagine sono segnate.	Tengo un libro que lo explica de varias formas; las páginas están señaladas.
(Shay an leevr kee andeek toot lay pozeesyon; shett an koo dei, shay markay lay pash.)	*(Oh oon mah-noo-ah-leh keh in-seh-nyaa meh-to-dee divers-ee; leh pa-jee-neh sono se-nya-teh.)*	*(Téngoh oon leebroh ké loh explekah deh báreeyas fórmass; lass páhhenass stán sehnyaládass.)*

C'est toi qui a écrit ça?	L'hai scritto tu?	¿Lo escribiste tu?
(Say twar kee ar aikree sah?)	*(Lah-ee scree-toh too?)*	*(Loh screebeesteh too?)*

I am a Press photographer; may I take your picture?

Ich bin Pressefotograf; darf ich von Ihnen eine Aufnahme machen?

(Ish bin presse-fotograaf, daarf ish fon ihnen yne aofnaame maachen?)

Just lift your skirt a bit so I can get a shot of your lovely legs.

Den Rock ein bisschen höher bitte, damit Ihre schönen Beine ganz auf's Bild kommen.

(Den rock yn biss-shen hoeher, bitte, daamit ihre shoenen byne gans aof's bild kommen.)

Actually I work for "Playboy"; how about a picture for them?

Ich arbeite ja eigentlich für "Playboy"; wie wär's mit einer Aufnahme für die Zeitschrift?

(Ish arbyte yaa ygentlish fuer Playboy; vi vair's mit yner aofnaame fuer di tsytshrift?)

I prefer nude photography because the texture of female flesh is so expressive.

Am liebsten mache ich Aktaufnahmen, weil die weibliche Haut so ausdrucksvoll ist.

(Am liebsten maache ish aaktaofnaamen, vyl di vyblishe haot zo aosdrooks-foll ist.)

FRENCH	ITALIAN	SPANISH

Je suis reporter photo-graphe, je peux vous prendre une photo?

(Sher swee rehportair-photo-grahf, sher per voo prandr in photaw?)

Sono un foto-reporter. Posso fotografarla?

(Sono oon foto-reporter. Posoh photo-gra-pharlah?)

Soy fotógrafo de prensa, ¿puedo sacarte una foto-grafía?

(Sóy photógrahfoh deh prén-sah, pwéddoh sahkárrteh oonah photographyah?)

Soulevez un peu la jupe que je puisse photographier ces belles jambes que vous avez!

(Soolvay an per la ship kersh pweece photografyay say bell shamb ker voo zavay!)

Alzi un po' la gonna; vorrei mettere in risalto le sue meravigliose gambe.

(Ahltzee oon poh lah goh-nah; voray meh-tehreh in ree-sahl-to leh sweh meh-rahvee-lyoseh gahm-beh.)

Levántate un poquito la falda para que pueda retra-tar tus bonitas piernas.

(Lebántah-teh oon pokeetoh lah fáldah párah ké pwéddah rehtrah-tárr toos boneetass peeyernass.)

En réalité, je travaille pour Playboy; ça vous dirait de poser pour ce magazine?

(An raiahleetay, sher travaee poor Playboy; sah voo deeray der pozay poor ser magazeen?)

Lavoro per la rivista Play-boy—vorrei pubblicare una sua fotografia.

(Lah-voro per lah ree-veesta Playboy — voray poo-bleekah-reh oona swah photograph-ya.)

En realidad trabajo para Playboy, ¿qué te parece que te haga unas fotos para esta revista?

(En reh-ahleedád trahbáh-hoh párah Playboy, ké te parétheh ké teh ágah oonass phótoss párah éstah reh-beestah?)

Je préfère faire des nus, car les femmes ont une texture de peau si expres-sive!

(Sher preffair day ni, kahr lay famm ontin textir der paw see expresseev!)

Preferisco i nudi. Trovo la pelle femminile cosí foto-genica!

(Prefer-eeskoh ee noo-dee. Trovo lah peh-leh feh-mee-neeleh kosèe photogenic-ah.)

Prefiero la fotografía . de desnudo porque la textura de la carne femenina es tan expresiva . . .

(Prehfeeyéroh lah photo-graphyah deh dessnoodoh pór-ké lah textoorah deh lah kárneh fehmehneenah ess tán expressibah . . .)

ANYWHERE

My studio is at my flat.

Das Atelier ist in meiner Wohnung.

(Das aatelyeh ist in myner vonoong.)

This is a special camera that needs no film in it.

Das ist eine besondere Kamera, die braucht keinen Film.

(Das ist yne bezondere camera, di braocht kynen film.)

Don't be shy; think of me like a doctor.

Nicht so schüchtern; stell' Dir vor, ich bin Dein Arzt.

(Nisht zo shuesh-tern; shtell dir for ish bin dyn aartst.)

AT HER PARENTS

You're surely her sister, never her mother!

Sie sind doch bestimmt die Schwester, nicht die Mutter!

(Zi zind doch beshtimmt di shvester, nisht di mootter!)

What magnificent cooking!

Das schmeckt ja grossartig!

(Daass shmeckt yaa grossaartig!)

FRENCH	ITALIAN	SPANISH
Mon appartement me sert de studio. *(Mon apparterman mer sair der stidyaw.)*	Ho lo studio nel mio appartamento. *(Oh lo stoo-dio nehl mee-o ahpart-ahmento.)*	Tengo el estudio en mi piso. *(Téngoh el stood-yoh en mee peesoh.)*
C'est un appareil photo spécial qui n'a pas besoin de film. *(Settan apparay photaw spaisyal kee nah par berzwand feelm.)*	Questa è una macchina speciale: non ha bisogno di pellicola. *(Kwehstah eh oona makeenah speh-chah-leh. Non ah bee-sonyo dee pehlleekolah.)*	Es una cámara especial, que no necesita película. *(Ess oonah cámahrah spethiál, ké noh nethessíttah pehl-leekoolah.)*
Ne soyez pas intimidée, faites comme si j'étais votre docteur. *(Ner swayay par zanteemeeday, fait comm see shettay votr doctehr.)*	Non sia cosí timida. Faccia conto che io sia un medico. *(Non see-ah kosèe timid-ah. Fah-chah con-to keh yo see-ah oon meh-dee-ko.)*	No tengas vergüenza, piensa en mí como médico. *(Noh téngass behrg-wénthah, peeyénsah én mee kómoh médeekoh.)*
Je suis sûr que vous êtes sa sœur; pas sa mère, c'est impossible! *(Sher swee sir ker voo zait sa sehr; par sa mair, settam possible!)*	Ma lei è la sorella, non la mamma! *(Mah leh-ee eh lah sohrehl-lah, non lah mammah!)*	¡Usted debe de ser su hermana, y no su madre! *(Oostéd débeh deh sérr soo ehrmánah, ee noh soo máddreh!)*
Vous êtes un véritable cordon bleu! *(Voo zait an vaireetabl cordon blehr!)*	Che magnifico pranzo! *(Keh mah - nee - fee - koh prahn-tzoh!)*	¡Qué comida más exquisita! *(Ké kohmeedah máss exkeeseetah!)*

I earn very little.

Ich verdiene noch sehr wenig.

(Ish ferdine noch zehr venig.)

I'm only a student.

Ich bin ja nur Student.

(Ish bin yaa noor shtoodend.)

May I have some more of this marvellous dish?

Darf ich noch etwas von dieser köstlichen Speise haben?

(Daarf ish noch etvaas von dizer koestlishen shpyze haaben?)

I hope one day I may be worthy of your daughter.

Ich hoffe, ich werde Ihrer Tochter eines Tages wert sein.

(Ish hoffe, ish verde irer tochter ynes taages vert zyn.)

When exactly will you be away and for how long?

Wann fahren Sie fort? Auf wie lange?

(Van faahren zi fort? aof vi laange?)

I'm afraid I couldn't marry her, my wife would object.

Heiraten kann ich Ihre Tochter nicht; meine Frau würde entschieden dagegen sein.

(Hiraaten kaann ish ire tochter nisht; myne frao vuerde entshiden dagegen zyn.)

FRENCH	ITALIAN	SPANISH
Mon salaire est ridicule.	Guadagno assai poco.	Gano muy poco
(Mon sahlair ay reedeekil.)	*(Gwah-dah-nee-oh ahs-sah-ee poh-koh.)*	*(Gáhnoh mooy pókoh.)*
Je ne suis qu'un étudiant.	Sono ancora studente.	Sólo soy un estudiante.
(Shern swee kan aitidyan.)	*(Soh-noh ahn-ko-rah stooden-teh.)*	*(Sóloh sóy oon stoodeeyánteh.)*
Puis-je me servir encore de ce merveilleux plat?	Oso chiederle ancora un po' di questa pietanza squisita?	¿Puedo comer un poco más de este maravilloso plato?
(Pweesh mer sairveer ankor der ser mairvaiyehr plah?)	*(Oh-zoh kee-eh-der-leh ahn-ko-rah oon poh dee kwestah pee-eh-tan-zah skwee-zee-tah?)*	*(Pwéddoh kohmérr oon pókoh máss deh ésteh marah-beellyósoh plátoh?)*
J'espère être digne un jour votre fille.	Spero un giorno di dimostrarmi degno di sua figlia.	Espero que algún día sea digno de su hija.
(Shaispair aitr deen an shoor der votr feey.)	*(Speh-roh oon johr-noh dee dee-mostrar-mee deh-nee-oh dee soo-ah fee-lee-ah.)*	*(Spéroh ké algoon deeya séah deeknoh deh soo ee-hah.)*
A quelle date pensez-vous partir et pour combien de temps?	Quand'è che vanno via esattamente, e per quanto?	¿Cuándo se marchará usted y por cuánto tiempo?
(A kel dart pansay-voo parteer ay poor combyan der tam?)	*(Kwan-deh keh vahn-noh vee-ah eh-sah-tah-menteh eh per kwantoh tempoh?)*	*(Kwándoh seh marchahrá oostéd ee pór kwántoh tee-yémpoh?)*
J'ai bien peur de ne pouvoir l'épouser, ça ne plairait pas du tout à ma femme.	Temo che proprio non potrei sposarla: mia moglie si opporrebbe.	Siento mucho no poderme casar con ella. Mi mujer se opondría.
(Shay byan pehr der ner poovwahr laipoozay, sahn plairay par di too ar ma famm.)	*(Teh-moh keh proh-pree-oh non poh-treh-ee spoh-sarlah: mee-ah moh-lee-eh see op-por-rehb-beh.)*	*(Seeyéntoh mootchoh noh podérr-meh kahssárr kón ehllya. Mee moohhérr sé opondreeyah.)*

IN THE CAR

These tip back seats are very comfortable.

Diese Liegesitze sind sehr bequem.

(Dize ligezitse zind zehr bequaym.)

Let me fix your safety-belt.

Komm, ich schnalle Deinen Sicherheitsgurt fest.

(Komm, ish shnaalle dynen zisherhytsgoort fest.)

Move your seat back, it's easier.

Es geht leichter, wenn Du Deinen Sitz zurückschiebst.

(Es gayt lyshter, venn doo dynen zits tsoorueck-shibst.)

The gear shift doesn't leave my hand much room.

Die Schaltung lässt nicht viel Platz für meine Hände.

(Di shaaltoong laysst nisht fil plaats fuer myne haynde.)

I'm sorry, my watch has caught in your garter while I was changing gear.

Entschuldige, beim Schalten ist meine Uhr in Deinem Strumpfband hängen geblieben.

(Entshooldige, bym shaalten ist myne oor in dynem shtroomfbaand hayngen gebliben.)

FRENCH	ITALIAN	SPANISH
Ces sièges-couchettes sont très confortables.	Questi sedili ribaltabili sono comodissimi.	Éstos asientos abatibles son muy confortables.
(Say syaish-cooshett son tray confortahbl.)	*(Kweh-stee sehdee-lee ree-bahltah-beelee sono como-dee-see-mee.)*	*(Èstoss assyéntoss ahbah-teeb-less són mooy com-fortáb-less.)*
Je vais vous mettre la ceinture de sécurité.	Lasci che le agganci la cintura di sicurezza.	Déjame que te abroche el cinturón de seguridad.
(Sher vay voo metr la santir der saikireetay.)	*(Lah-shee keh leh ah-gahn-chee lah cheen-too-rah dee see-kooretza.)*	*(Déhhah-meh ké teh ah-brótcheh él thintoorón deh segooreedád.)*
Poussez votre siège vers l'arrière, vous serez mieux.	Sposti indietro il sedile, è piú facile.	Echa el asiento hacia atrás, es más fácil.
(Poossay votr syaish vair laryair, voo sray myer.)	*(Spost-ee in-dee-ehtro eel seh-dee-leh, eh pew fah-chee-leh.)*	*(Étchah él assyéntoh átheeya ahtráss, ess máss fáthill.)*
Le changement de vitesses ne laisse pas beaucoup de liberté à ma main.	La leva del cambio non mi permette di muovere la mano.	La palanca de cambio no me deja mucho sitio para la mano.
(Ler shanshman der veetaiss ne laiss par bawkood lee-bairtay ar ma man.)	*(Lah leh-vah dehl cahm-bee-o non mee perm-eh-teh dee moo-oh-vehre lah mah-no.)*	*(Lá pahlánkah deh kám-beeyoh noh meh déhhah mootchoh síttyoh párah lá mánoh.)*
Je m'excuse, ma montre s'est accrochée à votre jarretelle pendant que je changeais de vitesse.	Mi dispiace, mi si è impi-gliato l'orologio nella sua giarrettiera mentre cam-biavo marcia.	Lo siento, se me ha en-ganchado el reloj con tu liga al cambiar de marcha.
(Sher mexkiz, ma montr say takroshay ar votr shartel pandan ker sher shanshayd veetaiss.)	*(Mee dis-pee-a-cheh, mee see eh eem-pee-lee-ah-to l'oroh-lojo neh-la swa jareh-tee-ehrah mehntreh cahm-bee-ahvo march-ah.)*	*(Loh seeyéntoh, seh mé ah engantchádoh él rhelóhh kón too leegah ál kambeeyárr deh márchah.)*

There's plenty left when it shows empty.

Es gibt immer noch ziemlich viel, wenn der Zeiger auf "leer" steht.

(Es gibt immer noch tsimlish fiel, venn der tsyger aof "layr" shteht.)

I've run out of petrol.

Aber jetzt ist der Tank leer.

(Aaber yetst ist der taank layr.)

The car has broken down.

Der Wagen liegt fest.

(Der vaagen ligt fest.)

We're miles from anywhere.

Da ist weit und breit nichts in Aussicht.

(Daa ist vyt oond bryt nishts in aosisht.)

It's my fault you are so cold, the least I can do is get you warm.

Es ist meine Schuld, dass Dich so friert, kann ich Dich wenigstens ein bisschen erwärmen.

(Es ist myne shoold, daas dish zo frirt, kan ish dish venigstens yn bis-shen ervairmen.)

Ne vous inquiétez pas, il y a encore plein d'essence dans le réservoir quand la jauge indique zéro.

(Ner voo zankyetay par, eelyar ankor plun daissans dan ler raizairvwahr kan la shawsh andeek zairo.)

Anche quando segna zero c'è ancora una grossa riserva.

(Ahnkeh kwando seh-nya zeh-ro chay ahn-kó-ra oona gross-ah ree-servah.)

Todavía queda mucha, cuando parece que está vacío.

(Toddabeeyah kéddah mootchah, kwándoh parétheh ké stáh bahtheeyoh.)

Zut, je n'ai plus d'essence!

(Zit, sher nay pli daissans!)

Non c'è piú benzina.

(Non chay pew benzee-nah.)

Me he quedado sin gasolina.

(Meh eh keddádoh sinn gassoleenah.)

Il ne manquait plus que ça, on est tombé en panne!

(Eel ner mankay plik sah, onay tombay an pann!)

S'è guastata la macchina.

(Seh gwah-stata lah makeena.)

El coche está averiado.

(El kótcheh stáh abereeyádoh.)

On est en pleine cambrousse.

(Onay tan plenn cambrooce.)

Non c'è nulla qui vicino.

(Non chay noo-lah kwee vee-chee-no.)

Estamos lejos de cualquier sitio.

(Stámoss léhhoss deh kwalkeeyer síttyoh.)

Pauvre chou! vous avez froid; comme tout ça est de ma faute, le moins que je puisse faire est de vous tenir chaud.

(Pawvr shoo! voo zavay frwar; comm too sah sayd ma fawt, ler mwan kersh pweece fair ay der voo terneer shaw.)

È colpa mia se hai tanto freddo: il minimo che posso fare è scaldarti.

(Eh colpah mee-ah seh ah-y tahnto freh-do, eel meeneemo keh posso far-reh eh skahl-dartee.)

Es culpa mía que tengas tanto frío; lo menos que puedo hacer es calentarte.

(Ess koolpah meeah ké téngass tántoh freeoh; loh ménoss ké pwéddoh atherr ess kahlentarr-teh.)

IN THE CAR

How do you unfasten these things?

Wie machst Du diese Dinger auf?

(Vi machst doo dize dinger aof?)

It's all right, officer; we were just studying the map.

Schon gut, Herr Wachtmeister, wir studieren gerade die Strassenkarte.

(Shon good, Herr vachtmyster, vir shtoodiren geraade di shtraasenkaarte.)

IN THE BUS

I'm so sorry, I thought it was the strap.

Verzeihen Sie, ich dachte es war die Strippe zum festhalten.

(Fertsyn zi, ish dachte es vaar di shtrippe tsoom festhaalten.)

No, I didn't pinch it.

Ich habe die Strippe nicht gekniffen.

(Ish haube dee shtrippe nisht gekkniffen.)

How far can I go for fourpence?

Wie weit kann man für zwanzig Pfennig fahren?

(Vi vyt kann maan fuer tsantsig pfennig faaren?)

FRENCH	ITALIAN	SPANISH
Comment est-ce que vous défaites ça? *(Comman esker voo deffait sah?)*	Come si fa a slacciare qui? *(Cohmeh see fah ah slah-chahreh kwee?)*	¿Cómo se aflojan estas cosas? *(Kómoh sé ahflóhhan éstass kóssas?)*
Ça va, m'sieur l'agent, on regardait simplement la carte. *(Sah var, m'sier larshan, on r'gahrday samplman la cart.)*	Stiamo soltanto studiando la carta stradale, signor vigile. *(Stee-ahmo sol-tahnto stoo-dee-ahndo lah car-tah strah-dah-leh, see-nior vee-jee-leh.)*	¡Está bien, guardia! Sólo estábamos mirando el mapa. *(Stáh beeyén, gwárdyah! Sóloh stábahmoss meerándoh él mápah.)*
Je m'excuse, je voulais simplement m'attraper à la barre pour ne pas tomber. *(Sher mexkiz, sher voolay samplman matrappay ar la bar poor ner par tombay.)*	Scusi, credevo fosse la maniglia. *(Skoo-see, kreh-deh-vo foh-se lah mah-nee-lee-ah.)*	Lo siento, creí que era un agarradero. *(Loh seeyéntoh, kreeh-ee ké érah oon ahgahrrahdéroh.)*
Pas du tout, ce n'est pas moi! *(Par di too, snay par mwar!)*	No, non le ho dato un pizzicotto. *(Noh, non leh oh dah-to oon pee-tzee-cohto.)*	No, yo no he sido. *(Noh, yoh noh eh seedoh.)*
Jusqu'où peut-on aller pour vingt centimes? *(Shiskoo perton allay poor van santeem?)*	Fin dove posso arrivare con questo biglietto? *(Feen doveh possoh ah-ree-vahreh con kwesto bee-lee-ehto?)*	¿Hasta dónde puedo ir por dos pesetas? *(Ástah dóndeh pwéddoh eer pór dóss pessétass?)*

IN THE BUS

In my country rubbing knees is a simple sign of courtesy.

Wo ich herkomme, da ist das Kniereiben ein Ausdruck der Höflichkeit.

(Vo ish herkomme, daa ist das kkniryben yn aosdrook der hoeflishkyt.)

IN THE COUNTRY

Let's pick bluebells/roses/daisies/weeds.

Komm, wir pflücken Glockenblumen / Rosen / Gänseblümchen / Unkraut.

(Komm, vir pfluecken glockenbloomen | rozen | gaynzeblumshen | oonkraot.)

I'm a plain-clothed customs officer and believe you are hiding contraband on your person.

Ich bin Zollbeamter in Zivil; ich glaube, Sie haben Schmuggelware an sich.

(Ish bin tsollbe-aamter in tsivil; ish glaobe, zi haaben shmoogelvaare aan zish.)

Let's sit down on this hayrick.

Setzen wir uns doch in den Heuschober.

(Zetsen vir oons doch in den hoyshober.)

FRENCH	ITALIAN	SPANISH
Dans mon pays, la politesse veux qu'on se touche les genoux.	Al mio paese, toccare il ginocchio è un segno di elementare cortesia.	En mi país frotarse las rodillas es una mera señal de cortesía.
(Dan mon paiee, la poleetess ver konce toosh lay shernoo.)	*(Ahl mee-o pah-ehseh toh-kah-reh eel jee-nock-eeo eh oon seh-neeo dee element-ahreh cohr-teh-seeah.)*	*(Én mee pah-is frohtárr-seh lass rhodeellyass ess oonah mérah senyáll de cohrteh-síah.)*
Allons cueillir des jacinthes — roses — marguerites — herbes folles.	Cogliamo le violette/le rose/ le margherite/ le erbacce.	Cojamos campanillas, rosas, margaritas y hierbecillas.
(Allon keryeer day shasant — rawz — marguereet — airb fol.)	*(Co-lee-amo leh vee-ohleh-teh/leh roseh/leh mar-gueh-ree-teh/leh ehrbah-cheh?)*	*(Kohhámoss kampahn-eellyass/róssass/margareetass ee yerbehthillyass.*
Je suis douanier en civil et je veux vérifier si vous n'avez pas sur vous de la contrebande.	Sono un doganiere in bor-ghese e ho motivo di ritenere che nasconda ad-dosso materiale di contrab-bando.	Soy un vista de Aduanas de paisano, y creo que lleva contrabando encima.
(Sher swee dooanyay an seeveel ay sher ver vaireefyay see voo navay par sir voo der la kontrband.)	*(Sonoh oon doh-gah-nee-eh-reh in bor-ghe-seh eh oh motiv-oh dee ree-tehneh-reh keh nah-skon-dah ah-dohso mah-teh-ree-ahleh dee cohn-trah-bahndo.)*	*(Sóy oon beestah de Ad-wánass deh paysánnoh y kréoh ke llyévah contra-bándoh entheemah.)*
Oh la belle meule de foin! Allons nous y asseoir un peu.	Sediamoci su questo fienile.	Sentémonos en este pajar.
(Oh la bell merl der fwan! Allon noo zee asswahr an per.)	*(Seh - dee - ahmochee soo kwestoh fee-ehnee-leh.)*	*(Sentémonoss en ésteh pah-hárr.)*

IN THE COUNTRY

Let's walk there away from the crowd into that lovely long grass.

Gehen wir doch da drüben in das schöne, hohe Gras, weit weg von den vielen Menschen.

(Gayn vir doch daa drueben in das shoene, hohe graass, vyt vayg fon den filen menshen.)

An insect has gone down your blouse—let me help you.

Ein Käfer ist gerade in Deine Bluse gekrabbelt, aber ich werde ihn schon finden.

(Yn kayfer ist geraade in dyne bloose gecrabbelt, aber ish verde ihn shon finden.)

Lying down is the only way to appreciate the sky.

Im Liegen kann man erst den Himmel richtig geniessen.

(Im liegen kann maan erst den himmel rishtig geniessen.)

There's nobody about and it's the only real way to swim.

Hier ist doch kein Mensch, so schwimmt man besser.

(Hir ist doch kyn mensh, zo shvimt maan besser.)

Si on quittait toute cette foule pour aller marcher dans cette belle prairie?

(See on keetay toot set fool poor allay marshay dan set bell prairee?)

Allontaniamoci da tutta questa gente; andiamo a passeggiare tra quella bella erba alta.

(Ah-lontah-nee-ah-mochee dah too-tah kwestah jenteh; ahn-dee-ahmo ah passeh-jah-reh tra kwelah bellah eh-rbah ah-ltah.)

Huyamos de la multitud y vámonos a aquel prado de hierba alta.

(Ooyámoss de la moolteetood ee bámonoss ah ahkéll prádoh deh yérbah áltah.)

Oh là! il y a une petite bête qui est entrée sous votre chemisier; attendez, je vais la sortir.

(Oh lar! eelyar in pteet bet kee ay tantray soo votr shmeezyay; attanday, sher vay la sorteer.)

Ho visto un insetto correre dentro alla sua camicetta— l'aiuto a cercarlo.

(Oh vee-sto oon inset-toh coh-reh-reh dehntro ah-lah swah cah-mee-cheh-tah — l'ah-yew-toh ah cher-carloh.)

Se te ha metido un insecto bajo la blusa, déjame que te lo saque.

(Seh teh ah meteedoh oon eenséktoh báhhoh lah bloossah, déhhahmeh ké teh loh sákeh.)

Rien ne vaut de s'étendre sur le dos pour apprécier toute la beauté du ciel!

(Ryan ner vaw der setandr sir le do poor appressyay toot la bawtay di syell!)

È solo sdraiati che si può vedere bene il cielo.

(Eh solo sdrah-yah-tee keh see pwoh veh-deh-reh beneh eel chay-lo.)

La única forma de contemplar el cielo es acostándose.

(Lah ooneekah formah deh kohntemplárr él thiyéloh ess akosstándoseh.)

Il n'y a personne dans les parages et c'est la meilleure façon d'aller dans l'eau.

(Eelnyar pairsonn dan lay parahsh ay say la meyehr farson dallay dan law.)

Siamo proprio soli ed è il miglior modo per nuotare.

(See-ahmo pro-pree-oh solee ehd-ay eel mee-leeor modo per noo-oh-tar-eh.)

No hay nadie por aquí, y esta es la única forma verdadera de nadar.

(Noh áy náddyeh pór akee, ee éstah ess lah ooneekah fórmah berdahdérah deh naddarr.)

IN THE COUNTRY

You do look cold—let me get you warm.

Du siehst verfroren aus—komm, ich wärme Dich.

(Doo ziest ferfroren aos, komm, ish vairme dish.)

Where I come from we are modern about these things.

Da wo ich herkomme, denkt man über diese Dinge sehr modern.

(Da vo ish herkomme, denkt maan ueber diese dinge zehr modairn.)

I have a groundsheet in case the grass is wet.

Ich habe eine Decke, falls das Gras nass ist.

(Ish haabe yne decke, falls das graass nass ist.)

AT THE PARTY

There's no food left—but here is a large drink instead.

Zu Essen gibt's nicht mehr—aber trinken Sie doch.

(Tsoo ayssen gibt's nisht mayr—aber trinken zi doch.)

Are you over sixteen?

Sie sind doch schon sechzehn?

(Zi zind doch shon zaysh-tsehn?)

FRENCH	ITALIAN	SPANISH

On dirait que vous avez froid; je vais vous réchauffer un peu.

(On deerayk voo zavay frwar; sher vay voo raishawfay an per.)

Si vede che hai freddo. Ti scaldo io.

(See veh-deh keh ah-y frehdo. Tee scah-ldoh ee-oh.)

Creo que tienes frío. Déjame que te caliente.

(Kréoh ké teeyénness freeyoh. Déhhah-meh ké teh kaleeyénteh.)

Dans mon pays, on n'est pas vieux jeu; on a des idées modernes à ce sujet.

(Dan mon paiee, onay par vyer sher; on ar day zeeday modairn ass sishay.)

Al mio paese in queste cose siamo molto moderni.

(Ahl mee-oh pah-ehseh in kweh-steh coseh see-ahmo molto modern-ee.)

De donde yo vengo, somos modernos en estas cosas.

(Deh dóndeh yoh béngoh, sómoss modérnoss én éstass kóssas.)

J'ai un tapis de sol, au cas où l'herbe est mouillée.

(Shay an tapee der sol, aw car oo lairb ay mooyay.)

L'erba è bagnata, ho portato apposta un impermeabile.

(L'ehrbah eh ba-nee-ahtah, oh port-ahto ah-postah oon impehr-meh-ahbee-leh.)

Tengo una esterilla por si la hierba está húmeda.

(Téngoh oonah stehreellyah pór see lah yérbah stáh oomehdah.)

Il n'y a plus rien à manger, mais prenez un bon verre à la place.

(Eelnyar pli ryenar manshay, may prernay an bon vair ar la plahs.)

Da mangiare non è rimasto nulla, ma bevi questo invece.

(Dah mahn-jah-reh non eh ree-mah-sto noo-lah, mah beh-vee kwehsto in-vehcheh.)

No ha quedado comida, pero en cambio hay mucho para beber.

(Noh ah kehdádoh komeedah, péroh en kámbeeyoh áy mootchoh párah behberr.)

Je parie que vous n'avez même pas seize ans!?

(Shparee ker voo navay maim par saix an!?)

Ha già compiuto 16 anni?

(Ah jah com-pew-to sehdee-chee ah-nee?)

¿Ha cumplido los dieciséis años?

(Ah koompleedoh lóss dyéthisséis ányoss?)

AT THE PARTY

My uncle Mr. Rockefeller always says . . .	Mein Onkel Rockefeller sagt immer . . . *(Myn onkel Rockefeller saagt immer . . .)*
Let me take you home—my home.	Darf ich Sie zu mir nach Haus begleiten? *(Darf ish zi stoo mir nach haos beglyten?)*
It's quieter upstairs in the bedroom.	Oben im Schlafzimmer ist es viel ruhiger. *(Oben im shlaaftsimmer ist es fiel roohiger.)*
You have an incredible figure, surely it's not natural?	Sie haben ja eine tolle Figur; fast schon unnatürlich. *(Zi haaben yaa yne tolle figoor; fast shon oonaatuerlish.)*
Prove it.	Beweisen! *(Bevysen!)*
I know some grown-up games.	Ich kenne ein paar Spiele für Erwachsene. *(Ish kenne yn paar shpiele fuer ervaaxene.)*

FRENCH	ITALIAN	SPANISH
Mon oncle, Monsieur Rockefeller, disait toujours...	Mio zio, il signor Rockefeller, dice sempre che . . .	Mi tío, Mr. Rockefeller, siempre dice . . .
Mon onkl, Mersyer Rockfellair, deezay tooshoor...)	*(Mee-o tzee-o eel see-nyor Rockefeller, dee-cheh sehmpreh keh . . .)*	*(Mee tee-oh, Mr. Rockefeller, seeyémpreh deetheh . . .)*
Je vais vous ramener chez... moi.	Permetta che l'accompagni a casa—a casa mia.	¿Quiere que la lleve a casa . . . a mi casa?
(Sher vay voo ramnay shay... mwar.)	*(Per-meh-ta keh l'ah-kompah-nee ah cah-sah—ah cahsah mee-ah.)*	*(Keeyéreh. ké lah llyébeh ah kássah . . . ah mee kássah?)*
C'est plus calme en haut, dans la chambre à coucher.	È piú tranquillo in camera.	Arriba, en el dormitorio, se está más tranquilo.
(Say pli cahlm an aw, dan la shambr ar cooshay.)	*(Eh pew trahn-kwee-lo in camera.)*	*(Ah-ríbbah, én él dormeettórioh, sé stáh máss trahnkeeloh.)*
Vous avez un de ces corps, c'est incroyable! Jc parie que c'est du chiqué!	Ha un personale stupendo. Non mi dirà che è tutto naturale?	Tiene usted una silueta estupenda. A lo mejor no es natural.
(Voo zavay an der say kor, setancrwayabl! Sher paree ker say di shickay.)	*(Ah oon person-ah-leh stoopen-do. Non mee dee-rah keh eh too-to nah-too rahleh.)*	*(Teeyénneh oosté oonah siluet-tah stoopéndah. Ah loh mehhórr noh ess nattooral.)*
Chiche!	Me lo dimostri.	¡Demuéstrelo!
(Sheesh!)	*(Me lo dee-most-ree.)*	*(Dehmwéstreh-loh!)*
Je connais quelques passetemps pour adultes...	Conosco dei giuochi da adulti.	Sé algunos juegos para mayores.
(Shkonnay kelk passtan poor adilt...)	*(Co-no-sco day jew-okee dah ah-dooltee.)*	*(Sé ahlgoonoss hooéghoss párah mah-yóress.)*

AT THE DANCE

May I have the pleasure of this dance?

Darf ich um diesen Tanz bitten?
(Darf ish oom disen taans bitten?)

Oy, you'll do.

O—Sie sind o.k!
(o, zi zind o.k!)

Nice band, isn't it?

Die Kapelle ist gut, nicht wahr?
(Di kapelle ist good, nisht vaar?)

Do you come here often?

Sind Sie oft hier?
(Zind si oft hir?)

I'm sorry, my hand slipped.

Verzeihung, meine Hand ist gerutscht.
(Fertsy-oong, myne haand ist gerootsht.)

May I see you home?

Darf ich Sie nach Hause begleiten?
(Daarf ish zi naach haose beglyten?)

Let's go, kid.

Gehen wir, Kleine.
(Gehen vir, klyne.)

FRENCH	ITALIAN	SPANISH

M'accorderez-vous cette danse?

(Macordray-voo set dans?)

Posso avere il piacere di questo ballo?

(Possoh ah-veh-reh eel pee-ah-cheh-reh dee kwestoh bahl-loh?)

¿Me permites este baile?

(Meh permítess ésteh báyleh?)

Mmm... ça ira.

(Mmm... sar eerah.)

Su, andiamo?

(Soo, ahn-dee-ah-moh?)

¡Oh! Tú me vas.

(Oh! Too meh báss.)

Il est bien l'orchestre, n'est-ce pas?

(Eel ay byan lorchestr, naispar?)

Bell'orchestrina, no?

(Behl - lor - keh - streenah, noh?)

Buena orquesta, ¿verdad?

(Bwénah orkessta, berdath?)

Vous venez souvent ici?

(Voo vnay soovan eecee?)

Lei viene qui spesso?

(Leh-ee vee-eh-neh kwee speh-soh?)

¿Vienes a menudo por aquí?

(Beeyénness ah mehnoodoh pór akee?)

Oh, pardon! ma main a glissé...!

(Oh, pardon! ma man ar gleessay...!)

Scusi, mi è scivolata la mano.

(Skoo-zee, mee eh shee-voh-lah-tah lah mah-noh.)

Lo siento. Me ha resbalado la mano.

(Loh seeyéntoh. Meh ah ressbahládoh lah mánoh.)

Puis-je vous raccompagner chez vous?

(Pweesh voo racompanyay shay voo?)

Posso accompagnarla a casa?

(Possoh ak-kom-pah-nee-ar-lah ah kah-sah?)

¿Puedo Acompañarte a casa?

(Pwéddoh akompanyarrteh ah kássah?)

Allez, viens, Poupée!

(Allay, vyan, Poopay!)

Andiamo via, bambola.

(Ahn-dee-ah-moh vee-ah, bahm-bolah.)

¡Vámonos, niña!

(Bámonoss, neenyah!)

AT THE DANCE

I'm not a good dancer but I like holding women.

Ich bin zwar kein guter Tänzer, aber ich halte gerne Frauen im Arm.

(Ish bin tsvar kyn gooter tayntser, aber ish haalte gairne fraon im arm.)

Dancing closer is so much more stylish.

Eng tanzen ist viel schicker.

(Eng tantsen ist fil shicker.)

It's too warm, let's go out for some air.

Es ist sehr warm hier; schnappen wir doch ein bisschen frische Luft draussen.

(Es ist zehr varm hir; schnaappen vir doch yn bis-shen frishe looft draossen.)

Let me get you a fruit juice or something.

Soll ich Ihnen einen Fruchtsaft oder so 'was ähnliches holen?

(Zol ish ihnen ynen froochtzaft oder zo 'vas aynlishes holen?)

Take your girdle off and have fun.

Zieh' Deinen Hüftgürtel aus und amüsiere Dich.

(Tsih dynen hueftguertel aos oond amuezire dish.)

FRENCH	ITALIAN	SPANISH
Je ne suis pas un as de la piste, mais, j'aime bien tenir une femme dans mes bras.	Non ballo bene, ma mi piace avere una donna tra la braccia.	No bailo muy bien, pero me gusta abrazar a las mujeres.
(Shern swee pazanass der la peest, may shaym byan terneer in famm dan may brah.)	*(Non bahl-loh beh-neh, mah mee pee-ah-cheh ah-veh-reh oo-nah don-nah trah leh brah-cha.)*	*(Noh báyloh mooy beeyén, péroh mé goostah abrathár ah lass moohhéress.)*
Danser corps à corps, ça a tellement plus de style.	È tanto piú elegante ballare stretti stretti.	Bailar muy juntos es más elegante.
(Dansay korakor, sar ar tellman pli der steel.)	*(Èh tahn-toh pew eleganteh bahl - lah - reh streht - tee streht-tee.)*	*(Baylár mooy hoontoss ess máss ellegánteh.)*
Il fait trop chaud, sortons un peu prendre l'air.	Fa troppo caldo, andiamo a prendere una boccata d'aria.	Hace mucho calor; salgamos a tomar el fresco.
(Eel fay tro shaw, sorton an per prandr lair.)	*(Fah trop-poh kahl-doh, ahn-dee-ah-moh ah prendeh-reh oo-nah bok-kah-tah dah-reeah.)*	*(Atheh mootchoh kahlór; salgámoss ah tohmár él frésskoh.)*
Voulez-vous un jus de fruit ou une boisson quelconque...?	Permetta che le offra una spremuta o qualche altra cosa?	¿Quieres un zumo de frutas o algo?
(Voolay-voo an shi der frwee oo in bwahson kelkonk...?)	*(Permeht-tah keh leh offrah oo-nah spreh-moo-tah oh kwal-keh ahl-trah koh-sah.)*	*(Keeyéress oon thoomoh dé frootass oh álgoh?)*
Enlève donc ta gaîne et mets-toi à l'aise!	Si metta in libertà e si diverta.	Quítate el cinturón y te sentirás mejor.
(Anlaiv donk ta gain ay may-twar ar laiz!)	*(See met-tah een lee-bertàh eh see dee-vehr-tah.)*	*(Keetáteh él thintoorón ee teh senteeráss mehhór.)*

AT THE DANCE

But one's hand has to be there in this dance.

Bei diesem Tanz muss die eine Hand da sein.

(By disem tants moos di yne haand daa syn.)

Let me teach you a special dance.

Soll ich Dir einen ganz tollen Tanz beibringen?

(Zol ish dir ynen gaans tollen tants bybringen?)

GAMBLING

My name is ...... I've just won you.

Meine Name ist ...... ich habe Sie gerade gewonnen.

(Myn naame ist ...... Ish haabe zi geraade gevonnen.)

Let's play strip poker.

Spielen wir Strip-Poker.

(Shpielen vir strip-poker.)

Let's play strip pontoon.

Spielen wir Strip-Vingt-et-un.

(Shpielen vir strip-vingt-ay-ong.)

FRENCH	ITALIAN	SPANISH
Pour cette danse, il faut qu'une main soit placée en cet endroit. *(Poor set dans, eel faw kin man swar playsay an set andrwar.)*	Ma in questo ballo bisogna tenere una mano lí. *(Mah een kewstoh bahl-loh bee-zoh-neeah teh-neh-reh oo-nah mah-noh lée.)*	En este baile, una mano debe ponerse aquí. *(Enn ésteh báyleh, oonah mánoh débeh ponérseh akee.)*
Je vais vous apprendre un genre spécial de danse. *(Sher vay voo zaprandr an shanr spaisyal der dans.)*	Lasci che le insegni un ballo speciale. *(Lah-shee keh leh een-seh-nee oon bahl-loh speh-chee-ah-leh.)*	¿Quieres que te enseñe un nuevo baile? *(Keeyéress ké té ensényeh oon nwéboh báyleh?)*
Je m'appelle . . . . . . Je viens de vous gagner au jeu. *(Sher mappell . . . . . . Sher vyan der voo ganyay aw sher.)*	Mi chiamo . . . . . . e ho vinto lei come premio. *(Mee kee-ah-mo . . . . . . eh o veen-to lay comeh prehmee-o.)*	Me llamo . . . . . . y acabo de ganarla a usted. *(Meh llyámoh . . . . . . ee ahkáboh deh gahnárr-lah ah oostéh.)*
Si on faisait un strip-poker? *(See on ferzay an streeppokair?)*	Giuochiamo a poker con lo spogliarello. *(Jew-oh-kee-ah-mo ah poker kon lo spo-lee-ah-rehlo.)*	Juguemos al poker con nuestra ropa. *(Hoogémoss ál poker kón nwéstrah rópah.)*
Si on faisait une partie de strip-vingt-et-un? *(See on ferzay in partee der streep-vantai-an?)*	Giuochiamo a sette e mezzo con lo spogliarello. *(Jew-oh-kee-ah-mo ah sehteh eh meh-tzo kon lo spo-lee-ah-rehlo.)*	Juguemos al pontoon con nuestra ropa. *(Hoogémoss ál pontoon kón nwéstrah rópah.)*

GAMBLING

Let's play strip rummy.

Spielen wir Strip-Rommé.

(Shpielen vir strip-rommey.)

Let's play strip bridge.

Spielen wir Strip-Bridge.

(Shpielen vir strip-bridge.)

Let's play strip canasta.

Spielen wir Strip-Canasta.

(Shpielen vir strip-canasta.)

Let's play strip snap.

Spielen wir Strip-Schnipp-schnapp.

(Shpielen vir strip-shnipp-shnapp.)

No you can't have them back.

Nein, die Sachen kriegen Sie nicht wieder.

(Nyn, di zaachen kriegen zi nisht vieder.)

FRENCH	ITALIAN	SPANISH

Faisons une partie de strip-rummy.

(Ferzon in partee der streep-rimmee.)

Giuochiamo a ramino: chi perde si spoglia.

(Jew-oh-kee-ah-mo ah rah-mee-no. Kee pehr-deh see spo-leeah.)

Juguemos a strip-rummy.

(Hoogémoss ah streep rameeh.)

On va faire une partie de strip-bridge!

(On var fair in partee der streep-breedge!)

Giuochiamo a bridge: chi perde si spoglia.

(Jew - oh - kee - ah - mo ah bridge. Kee pehr-deh see spo-leeah.)

Juguemos al bridge con nuestra ropa.

(Hoogémoss ál bridge kón nwéstrah rópah.)

Sie on faisait un strip-canasta?

(See on ferzay an streep-canastah?)

Giuochiamo a canasta: chi perde si spoglia.

(Jew-oh-kee-ah-mo ah can-asta. Kee pehr-deh see spo-leeah.)

Juguemos a la canasta con nuestra ropa.

(Hoogémoss ah lah canasta kón nwéstrah rópah.)

Ça vous dirait de faire une partie de strip-snap?

(Sah voo deeray der fair in partee der streep-snap?)

Giuochiamo a rubamazzo: chi perde si spoglia.

(Jew-oh-kee-ah-mo ah roo-bah-mah-tzo. Kee pehr-deh see spo-leeah.)

Juguemos a strip-snap.

(Hoogémoss ah streep-snap.)

Je suis désolé, les vêtements enlevés ne se reprennent plus!

(Sher swee daizolay, lay vetman anlvay ner ser rerpren pli!)

No, non te li restituisco.

(No, non teh lee reh-stee-too-eesko.)

No, eso me lo quedo en prenda.

(Noh, éssoh meh loh kédoh en préndah.)

IN THE BAR

Is this seat taken?

Ist dieser Platz besetzt?
(Ist diser plaats bezetst?)

Two large gins, please.

Zwei doppelte Gin, bitte.
(Tsvy doppelte Gin, bitte.)

It's only a small one, nearly all fruit juice.

Das soll ein doppelter sein? Ist ja fast alles Fruchtsaft.
(Daas zoll yn doppelter zyn? ist yaa faast alles froochtsaaft.)

You're drinking very slowly.

Du trinkst ja sehr langsam.
(Doo trinkst yaa zehr laangzaam.)

We can both squeeze in over there.

Wir können uns da noch gerade zwischensetzen.
(Vir koennen oons daa nock geraade tsvishen zetsen.)

Let me steady you.

Kannst Dich an mich lehnen.
(Kannst dish aan mish laynen.)

Il y a quelqu'un à cette place? *(Eelyah kelkan ar set plahs?)*	È libero questo posto? *(Eh lee-beh-roh kwestoh poh-stoh?)*	¿Está ocupado este asiento? *(Stáh okoopádoh ésteh assyéntoh?)*
Deux grands gins, s'il vous plaît! *(Dehr gran gin, seel voo play.)*	Due doppi gin per favore. *(Doo-eh dop-pee gin per fah-voh-reh.)*	Dos ginébras dobles, por favor. *(Dóss heenébrass dób-less, pór fahbór.)*
Allez, c'est tout petit et il n'y a pratiquement que du jus de fruit. *(Allay, say too pertee ay eel nyah prateekman ker di shi der frwee.)*	Ma no, è quasi tutto succo di frutta. *(Mah noh, eh kwazee toot-toh sook-koh dee froot-tah.)*	Hay muy poquito, casi todo es zumo de frutas. *(Ay mooy pokeetoh, kássy tóddoh ess thoomoh dé frootass.)*
Vous buvez à peine et si lentement! *(Voo bivay ar pain ay see lantman.)*	Sta bevendo molto lentamente. *(Stah beh-vendoh moltoh len-tah-menteh.)*	Bebes muy despacio. *(Bébess mooy despáthioh.)*
Il y a là-bas une place pour nous deux, en nous serrant un peu. *(Eelyah lah-bah in plahs poor noo dehr, an noo serran an pehr.)*	Ci stiamo tutti e due in quell'angolino là. *(Chee stee-ah-moh toot-tee eh doo-eh een kwell an-goh-lee-noh lah.)*	Todavía cabemos los dos, estrechándonos un poco. *(Toddabíah kahbémoss lóss dóss, stretchándonoss oon pókoh.)*
Je vais vous soutenir. *(Sher vay voo sootneer.)*	Si appoggi a me. *(See ap-poh-jee ah meh.)*	Déjame que te aguante. *(Déhhah-meh ké teh agwánteh.)*

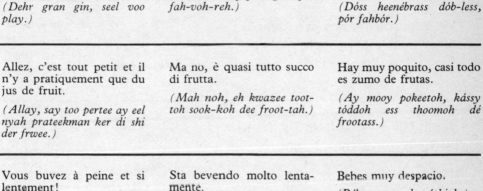

IN THE BAR

I always find beer best—it's cheaper too.

Am liebsten trinke ich Bier; ist auch billiger.

(Am libsten trinke ish beer; ist aoch billiger.)

Try a rum in your beer, dear.

Probiere doch 'mal einen Rum im Bier, Kleine.

(Probire doch 'maal ynen roomm im beer, klyne.)

Of course I'm not trying to get you tipsy.

Ich will Dir doch keinen Schwips andrehen!

(Ish vill dir doch kynen shvips andrehen!)

Now have something different.

Trinke 'mal etwas anderes.

(Trinke 'maak etvaas aanderes.)

I'd better see you safely home.

Ist wohl besser, wenn ich Dich nach Hause bringe.

(Ist vol besser, venn ish dish nach haoze bringe.)

FRENCH	ITALIAN	SPANISH
Je trouve que la bière, c'est ce qu'il y a de meilleur—et puis c'est bien moins cher! *(Sher troov ker la byair, say skeelyah der maiyehr—ay pwee say byan mwan shair.)*	Io preferisco sempre la birra—e costa anche meno. *(Ee - oh preh - feh - reeskoh sehm-preh lah beer-rah—eh koh-stah ahn-keh meh-noh.)*	Siempre me ha parecido mejor la cerveza . . . y más barata también. *(Seeyémpreh meh ah pare-theedoh mehhór lah zer-béthah . . . ee máss bahrátah tambeeyén.)*
Essayez donc un petit verre de rhum dans votre bière. *(Essayay donk an ptee vair der rom dan votr byair.)*	Aggiungiamo un po' di rum alla birra, cara. *(Ah-jewn-jah-moh oon poh dee room ahl-lah beer-rah, cah-rah.)*	Ponte un poquito de ron en la cerveza, querida. *(Pónteh oon pokeetoh deh rhón én lá zerbéthah, kehreedah.)*
Bien sûr que non, je ne cherche pas du tout à vous saoûler! *(Byan sir ker non, shern shairsh par di too ar voo sooluy!)*	Non è vero che sto cercando di ubriacarti. *(Non eh veh-roh keh stoh chair-can-doh dee oo-bree-ah-kartee.)*	Por supuesto, no trato de emborracharte. *(Pórr sooppwéstoh, noh tráttoh deh embohrrahchár-teh.)*
Prenez autre chose, maintenant. *(Prernay awtr shawz, mantnan.)*	Ora prendi qualcosa di diverso. *(Orah prehn-dee kwal-koh-zah dee dee-ver-soh.)*	Ahora probemos algo diferente. *(Ah-órah prohbémoss álgoh differénteh.)*
Il vaut mieux que je vous raccompagne jusque chez vous. *(Eel vaw myehr ker sher voo racompahn shisk shay voo.)*	Sarà meglio che l'accompagni a casa. *(Sarah meh-lee-oh keh lah-kom-pah-nee ah kah-sah.)*	Será mejor que te lleve a casa. *(Seráh mehhórr ké té llyébeh ah kásah.)*

PRESENTS FOR HER

Where is the ladies' underwear department?	Wo ist die Abteilung für Damen-unterwäsche? *(Vo ist di abtyloong fuer daamen-oonterwayshe?)*
Haven't you anything more interesting?	Haben Sie nichts interessanteres? *(Haaben zi nishts interessaanteres?)*
Bikini.	Bikini. *(Bikini.)*
See-through nightie.	Durchsichtiges Nachthemd. *(Doorsh-zishtiges naachthemd.)*
Transparent slip.	Hauchdünner Unterrock. *(Haochduenner oonterock.)*
G-string.	Eine Art Feigenblatt. *(Yne art fygenblatt.)*
Tassels.	Quasten. *(Quaasten.)*

FRENCH	ITALIAN	SPANISH

Où est le rayon des sous-vêtements féminins?

(Oo ayl rayon day soovetman faimeenan?)

Dov'è il reparto biancheria femminile?

(Dovéh eel reh-part-oh bee-ahn-key-ryah feh-mee-nee-leh?)

¿Dónde está el departamento de señoras?

(Dóndeh stáh el departahméntoh deh sehnyórass?)

Vous n'avez pas quelque chose de plus intéressant?

(Voo navay par kelk shawz der pli zanterressan?)

Non ha proprio nulla di piú interessante?

(Non ah propree-o noo-lah dee pew inter-eh-sahn-teh?)

¿No tiene algo más interesante?

(Noh teeyénne álgoh máss interehssánteh?)

Un bikini.

(An beekeenee.)

Bikini.

(Bikini.)

Bikini.

(Beekeenee.)

Une chemise de nuit transparente.

(In shmeez der nwee transpahrant.)

Una camicia da notte trasparente.

(Oona ˉ cah-mee-chah dah no-teh trah-spah-rehnteh.)

Camisones vaporosos.

(Kahmeessón-ness bapohrósoss.)

Une combinaison transparente.

(In combeenaizon transpehrant.)

Una sottoveste trasparente.

(Oona sotto-vest-eh trahspah-rehnteh.)

Bragas transparentes.

(Brágass transpahréntess.)

Un cache-sexe.

(An cash-sex.)

Minimum.

(Minim-oom.)

Taparrabos de vedette.

(Tahpah-rráboss deh vehdétteh.)

Des franfreluches.

(Day franfrerlish.)

Nappine.

(Nah-pee-neh.)

Borlas.

(Bórlass.)

PRESENTS FOR HER

Babydoll pyjamas.	Babydoll-Pyjamas. *(Babydoll-pyjamas.)*
Paste (jewellery).	Künstlicher Schmuck. *(Kuenstlisher shmoock.)*
Imitation diamonds.	Imitierte Diamanten. *(Imitirte diaamaanten.)*
Gold-plated star.	Vergoldeter Stern. *(Fergoldeter shtern.)*
Fancy garters.	Verzierte Strumpfbänder. *(Fertsirte shtroomfbender.)*
See-through panties.	Hauchdünne Höschen. *(Haochduenne hoes-shen.)*
Cut-away bra.	Tiefausgeschnittener B.H. *(Tief-aosgeshnittener bay haa.)*

FRENCH	ITALIAN	SPANISH
Un babydoll.	Babydolls.	Pijamas de muñequita.
(An babeedol.)	*(Babydolls.)*	*(Peehhámmass deh moon-yekeetah.)*
Du toc.	Bigiotteria.	Bisutería (joyería).
(Di tock.)	*(Bee-jot-err-yah.)*	*(Beessootery-ah (hoy-yery-ah).)*
Du strass.	Diamanti falsi.	Diamantes de imitación.
(Di strass.)	*(Dee-ah-mahntee fahl-see.)*	*(Deeahmántess deh imitah-thión.)*
Une broche en plaqué-or.	Una stella d'oro.	Estrellas doradas o plateadas.
(In brosh an plahkay-or.)	*(Oona steh-la doroh.)*	*(Stréhllyass dorádass oh plateh-ahdass.)*
Des jarretelles fantaisie.	Giarrettiere fantasia.	Ligas de fantasía.
(Day shartell fantaizee.)	*(Jar-reh-tee-ehreh fahn-tah-see-ah.)*	*(Lee-gass deh phantasy-ah.)*
Un slip transparent.	Mutandine trasparenti.	Pantaloncitos calados.
(An sleep transpahran.)	*(Moo-tahn-deeneh trah-spah-rehntee.)*	*(Pantahlonthitoss kaládoss.)*
Un balconet.	Reggiseno scollato.	Medios sostenes sin tirantes.
(An balkonay.)	*(Reh-jee-sehno skol-lah-to.)*	*(Mehddyoss sosténess seen teerántess.)*

PRESENTS FOR HER

Perfumes.	Parfüm. *(Paarfuem.)*
Bath essence.	Bade-Essenz. *(Baade-essence.)*

SOME USEFUL EXPRESSIONS

My wife doesn't understand me.	Meine Frau versteht mich nicht. *(Myne frao fershteht mish nisht.)*
Let me help you zip that up.	Komm, ich mache Dir den Zipp zu. *(Komm, ish maache dir dayn zipp tsoo.)*
It's all right; I'll sleep on the divan.	Das geht; ich schlafe auf dem Sofa. *(Das gayt; ish shlaafe aof dem sofa.)*
Only a cuddle.	Nur 'mal drücken. *(Noor 'maal druecken.)*

Du parfum.	Profumi.	Perfumes.
(Di parfam.)	*(Pro-foo-mee.)*	*(Perfoomess.)*

Essence de bain.	Essenze da bagno.	Colonia para el baño.
(Essans der ban.)	*(Essen-tzeh dah bah-nyo.)*	*(Kolóneeyah párah el bányoh.)*

Ma femme ne me comprend pas.	Mia moglie non mi capisce.	Mi mujer no me comprende.
(Ma famm ner mer kompran par.)	*(Mee-ah mo-lee-eh non mee cah-pee-sheh.)*	*(Mee moohhérr noh meh kompréndeh.)*

Laisse-moi te tirer ta fermeture-éclair.	Lasci che l'aiuti a chiudere la cerniera lampo.	Déjame que te abroche la cremallera.
(Laiss-mwar ter teeray ta fairmtir-ecklair.)	*(Lah-shee keh l'ah-yew-tee ah kew-deh-reh lah chair-nee-ehrah lahm-po.)*	*(Déhhah-meh ké teh ahbrótcheh lah crehmahllyérah.)*

D'accord, je dormirai sur le divan.	Non si preoccupi: io dormo sul divano.	Está bien. Dormiré en el diván.
(Dackor, sher dormeeray sir ler deevan.)	*(Non see preh-ohccoo-pee, yo dormoh sool dee-vahno.)*	*(Stáh beeyén. Dormeeréh én él deebán.)*

Simplement te prendre dans mes bras!	Solo un abbraccio.	Un abrazo solamente.
(Smplman ter prandr dan may brah!)	*(Solo oon ah-brah-choh.)*	*(Oon ahbráthoh solahménteh.)*

SOME USEFUL EXPRESSIONS

Honestly, I tried to book single rooms.

Wirklich, ich habe versucht, Einzelzimmer zu bekommen.

(Virklish, ish haabe ferzoocht, yntsel-tsimmer tsoo bekommen.)

This is a dangerous town, but I'll protect you.

Das ist eine ganz gefährliche Stadt, aber ich werde Dich beschützen.

(Das ist yne gaants gefairlishe shtadt, aber ish verde dish be-shuetsen.)

Let's try it another way.

Versuchen wir es doch einmal so.

(Ferzoochen vir es doch ynmaal zo.)

Your seams aren't straight.

Deine Nähte sind nicht gerade.

(Dyne nayte zind nisht geraade.)

I got carried away.

Ich konnte mich nicht ganz beherrschen.

(Ish konnte mish nisht gaans behairshen.)

Where is your birthmark?

Wo ist Dein Muttermal?

(Vo ist dyn mootter-maal?)

Je te jure, j'ai essayé de réserver des chambres à un lit!

(*Shter shir, shay essayay der raizairvay day shambr ar an lee!*)

Davvero, ho cercato di prenotare due camere separate.

(*Dah-vehro, oh chair-kahto dee preh-notah-reh doo-eh camereh sepa-rahteh.*)

¡Palabra! Quería alquilar habitaciones individuales.

(*Pahlábrah! Kehreeya ahlkeelárr ahbeetathióness eendeebeeduál-less.*)

C'est une ville de gangsters, mais je te protègerai.

(*Saitan veel der gangstair, may shter protaishray.*)

Questa è una città pericolosa, ma ti proteggo io.

(*Kwehsta eh oona chee-tàh per-ee-kolosa, mah tee proteh-goh yo.*)

Esta ciudad es peligrosa, pero yo te protegeré.

(*Estah thewdád ess pehlleegrósah, péroh yoh teh protehheréh.*)

Si on faisait ça d'une autre manière?

(*See on ferzay sah din awtr manyair?*)

Proviamo in un altro modo.

(*Pro-vee-ahmo in oon ahltro modo.*)

Probemos de otra manera.

(*Probbémoss deh ótrah mannérah.*)

Tes coutures ne sont pas droites!

(*Tay cootir ner son par drwat.*)

Hai la cucitura delle calze storta.

(*Ah-y lah koo-chee-too-rah deh-leh cahl-tzeh stor-tah.*)

Tus costuras no son rectas.

(*Toos costoorass noh són rréktass.*)

Je n'ai pas pu me contrôler!

(*Sher nay par pim controlay!*)

Ho perso la testa.

(*Oh per-so lah teh-stah.*)

He perdido los estribos.

(*Eh perdeedoh loss streebboss.*)

Montre-moi ton «envie».

(*Montr-mwar ton «anvee».*)

Dove hai un neo?

(*Doveh ah-y oon neh-o?*)

¿Dónde tienes otro lunar?

(*Dóndeh teeyénnes ótroh loonárr?*)

SOME USEFUL EXPRESSIONS

I'm afraid of the dark.	Ich fürchte mich im Dunkeln. *(Ish fuershte mish im doonkeln.)*
I am very rich.	Ich bin sehr reich. *(Ish bin zehr rysh.)*
Of course I'll write and send for you.	Natürlich schreibe ich Dir, wann Du nachkommen sollst. *(Natuerlish shrybe ish dir, van doo naachkommen zollst.)*
Never mind, I'll get you a new pair.	Macht ja nichts, ich kaufe Dir ein neues Paar. *(Macht yaa nishts, ish kaofe dir yn noyes paar.)*
Come over here.	Komm hier her. *(Komm hier hair.)*
Get undressed.	Zieh' Dich aus. *(Tsih dish aos.)*
Smith, spelled S–M–I–T–H.	Schmidt, buchstabiert S–C–H–M–I–D–T. *(Shmitt, boochshtabirt es-tsay-haa-em-i-day-tay.)*
I leave in the morning.	Ich fahre morgen Früh. *(Ish faare morgen frue.)*

FRENCH	ITALIAN	SPANISH

J'ai peur du noir!
(Shay pehr di nwahr.)

Ho paura del buio.
(Oh pah-oorah dehl boo-yo.)

Tengo miedo a la oscuridad.
(Téngoh meeyéddoh ah lah oskooreedád.)

Je suis très riche!
(Sher swee tray reesh!)

Io sono ricchissimo.
(Yo sono ree-kee-ssee-moh.)

Soy muy rico.
(Sóy mooy rickoh.)

Bien sûr que je t'écrirai pour te dire de venir.
(Byan sir kersh teckreeray poor ter deer der verneer.)

Certo che ti scriverò e ti farò venire.
(Chehr-to keh tee scree-vehròh eh tee fah-róh veh-nee-reh.)

Desde luego, te escribiré y te mandaré llamar.
(Désdeh lwégoh, teh scree-biréh ee teh mahndah-réh llyámárr.)

Ça ne fait rien, je t'achèterai une autre.
(Sarn fay ryan, sher tashetray in awtr.)

Non preoccupati, te ne compro un altro paio.
(Non pre-oc-coopahrtee, teh neh compro oon ahl-troh pah-yo.)

No importa, te compraré otro par.
(Noh eempórtah, teh com-prah-réh ótroh párr.)

Viens par ici.
(Vyan pahr eecee.)

Vieni qui.
(Vee-eh-nee kwee.)

Ven por aquí.
(Béhn pór akee.)

Déshabille-toi!
(Daizabeey-twar!)

Spogliati.
(Spoh-lee-ahtee.)

Desnúdate.
(Dessnoodah-teh.)

Je m'appelle Smith, S–M–I–T–H–
(Sher mapell Smith, ESS–EM–EE–TAY–ASH.)

Smith, che si scrive S–M–I–T–H–.
(Smith, keh see scree-veh S–M–I–T–H.)

Smith, deletreado S–M–I–T–H.
(Smith, dehlehtreh-ádoh S–M–I–T–H.)

Je pars demain matin.
(Sher pahr derman matan.)

Parto domattina.
(Part-oh do-mah-teenah.)

Me marcho por la mañana.
(Meh márchoh pór lá mahnyánah.)

SOME USEFUL EXPRESSIONS

I'm being sent on a secret mission with no address.	Ich habe einen Geheimauftrag, kann keine Adresse geben.
	(Ish haabe ynen gehym-aoftraag, kan kyne adresse gayben.)

FINDING OUT

Do you?	Willst Du? *(Villst doo?)*
Shall we?	Sollen wir? *(Zollen vir?)*
How about it?	Wie wär's? *(Vi vair's?)*
Let's?	Lass' uns doch. *(Laass oons doch.)*
Why not?	Warum nicht? *(Varoom nisht?)*
Try it.	Versuch's doch 'mal. *(Fersooch's doch 'maal.)*
When?	Wann? *(Vaan?)*
Where?	Wo? *(Vo?)*

FRENCH	ITALIAN	SPANISH

Je suis en mission secrète et je ne peux pas te donner d'adresse.

(Sher swee zan meesyon sercrett ay shern per par ter donnay dadress.)

Vado in missione segreta, senza indirizzo.

(Vah-do in miss-yo-neh seh-gretah sehn-tzah in-dee-ree-tzoh.)

Me mandan a una misión secreta, sin domicilio postal.

(Meh mándann ah oonah missión sehcrétah, seen domeethilioh postál.)

Alors...?

(Alor...?)

Vuoi?

(Voo-oh-ee?)

¿Quieres?

(Keeyéress?)

Oui...?

(Wee...?)

Vogliamo?

(Voh-lee-ah-moh?)

¿Lo haremos?

(Loh ahrémoss?)

Tu veux bien?

(Ti ver byan?)

Che ne diresti?

(Keh neh dee-reh-stee?)

¿Qué te parece?

(Ké teh pahrétheh?)

Allons, voyons...!

(Alon, vwahyon...!)

Sí?

(See?)

¿Vamos?

(Bámoss?)

Pourquoi pas?

(Poorkwar par?)

Perchè no?

(Per-kèh noh?)

¿Por qué no?

(Pór ké noh?)

Essaie!

(Essay!)

Prova.

(Proh-vah.)

¡Prueba!

(Prwébbah!)

Quand?

(Kan?)

Quando?

(Kwan-doh?)

¿Cuándo?

(Kwándoh?)

Où ça?

(Oo sah?)

Dove?

(Doh-veh?)

¿Dónde?

(Dóndeh?)

DECLARATIONS

Love you? Of course I love you, we're in bed again, aren't we?

Ob ich Dich liebe? Natürlich! Wir sind doch schon wieder im Bett, nicht wahr?

(Ob ish dish lihbe? naatuerlish! vir zind doch shon vider im bett, nisht vaar?)

You are so beautiful I don't trust myself alone with you.

Ich kann für nichts garantieren, wenn ich mit Dir allein bin—Du bist viel zu verführerisch.

(Ish kaan fuer nishts gaarantiren, ven ish mit Dir alyn bin—doo bist feel tsso ferfuererish.)

SLOPPY ENDEARMENT

Luscious bit of skirt.

Süsses Luder.

(Zuesses looder.)

Sugarpuss.

Zuckerpuppe.

(Tsoocker-pooppe.)

Honeybunch.

Affenschwänzchen.

(Aaffen-shvayns-shen.)

Apple of my eye.

Augapfel.

(Aogaap-fel.)

FRENCH	ITALIAN	SPANISH
Si je t'aime? Bien sûr que je t'aime! Ne suis-je pas en train de te le prouver encore une fois, dans ce lit? *(Seesh taim? Byan sir kersh taim! Ner sweesh pazan tran der terl proovay ankor in fwar, dan slee?)*	Se ti amo? Certo che ti amo, siamo di nuovo a letto insieme, no? *(Seh tee amoh? Chair-toh keh tee amoh, see-ah-moh dee noo-oh-voh ah let-toh eensee-eh-meh, noh?)*	¿Si te quiero? !Claro que te quiero! ¿No estamos otra vez en la cama? *(See teh keeyéroh? Clároh ké teh keeyéroh! Noh stámos ótrah béth én lá kámah?)*
Tu es si belle que je ne me fais pas confiance, seul avec toi. *(Ti ay see bell ker shern mer fay par confyans, serl aveck twar.)*	Lei è così bella che quando siamo soli ho paura di fare delle pazzie. *(Leh-ee eh ko-zée bella keh kwandoh see-ah-moh soh-lee oh pah-oo-rah dee fareh dehl-leh patzee-eh.)*	Eres tan bonita que no me fío de estar a solas contigo. *(Eres tán bohneetah ké noh meh feeyoh dé star ah sólas konteegoh.)*

FRENCH	ITALIAN	SPANISH
Petit bout de jupon. *(Pertee bood shipon.)*	Un bel pezzo di ragazza. *(Oon behl peh-tzo dee rah-gahtzah.)*	Perita en dulce. *(Pehreetah en doolzeh.)*
Mon minet en susucre. *(Mon meenay an sisikr.)*	Micina bella. *(Mee-chee-nah beh-lah.)*	Gatita linda. *(Gahteetah leendah.)*
Mon petit chou à la crème. *(Mon ptee shoo ar la craim.)*	Dolce tesoro. *(Dol-cheh teh-so-ro.)*	Cachito de miel. *(Katcheetoh deh meeyell.)*
Prunelle de mes yeux. *(Prinell der may zyer.)*	Pupilla dei miei occhi. *(Poo-pee-llah day mee-eh-ee okkee.)*	Niñita de mis ojos. *(Neenyeetah deh mees óhhoss.)*

SLOPPY ENDEARMENT

Heart's desire.

Herzenswunsch.
(*Hairtsens-voonsh.*)

Snooky pooky.

Schnuckiputzi.
(*Shnookki-poottsi.*)

Lovechick.

Betthäschen.
(*Betthays-shen.*)

Angel love.

Engelchen.
(*Angel-shen.*)

Gorgeous.

Bezaubernde.
(*Betsaobernde.*)

Raving beauty.

Grosse Schönheit.
(*Grosse shoenhyt.*)

Precious darling.

Goldstück.
(*Goldshtueck.*)

True love.

Grosse Liebe.
(*Grosse liebe.*)

Sweetie pie.

Süsse.
(*Zuesse.*)

FRENCH	ITALIAN	SPANISH
Amour de mon cœur. *(Amoor der mon ker.)*	Cuore mio. *(Coo-oh-reh mee-o.)*	Deseo de mi corazon. *(Dehseh-oh deh mee korahthón.)*
Chouchou chéri. *(Shooshoo shairee.)*	Coccolona. *(Co-cco-lo-nah.)*	Ratoncito mío. *(Rattonthítoh meeyoh.)*
Mon petit poulet. *(Mon ptee poolay.)*	Pulcino adorato. *(Pool-chee-no ah-dorah-to.)*	Palomita. *(Pahlohmeetah.)*
Mon ange. *(Mon ansh.)*	Angelo mio. *(Ahn-jeh-lo mee-o.)*	Angel de amor. *(Ahn-ghell deh ahmórr.)*
Madone. *(Mahdonn.)*	Seducente. *(Seh-doo-chen-teh.)*	Hermosa mía. *(Ermóssah meeyah.)*
Bcauté du diable. *(Bawtay di deeabl.)*	Bellezza rara. *(Beh-leh-tzah rah-rah.)*	Belleza delirante. *(Bellyéthah deliránteh.)*
Mon bijou. *(Mon beeshoo.)*	Gioia mia. *(Joy-ah mee-ah.)*	Mi bella amada. *(Mee béllyah ahmádah.)*
Amour de ma vie. *(Amoor de mar vee.)*	Unico amore. *(Oon-ee-ko ah-mo-reh.)*	Amor mío. *(Ahmórr meeyoh.)*
Mon sucre d'orge. *(Mon sikr dorsh.)*	Stellina. *(Steh-lee-nah.)*	Bombón. *(Bombón.)*

SLOPPY ENDEARMENT

Light of my life.	Meine Sonne. *(Myne zonne.)*
Darling.	Liebling. *(Liebling.)*
Precious.	Teures. *(Toyres.)*
Crumpet. ·	Puppe. *(Pooppe.)*
Lovey-dovey.	Flamme. *(Flamme.)*
Angel face.	Engelsgesicht. *(Engelsgesisht.)*
Lover girl.	Liebchen. *(Liebshen.)*
Whistlebait.	Kesse Biene. *(Kaysse biene.)*
The cat's whiskers.	Prachtstück. *(Pracht-shtueck.)*

FRENCH	ITALIAN	SPANISH
Lumière de ma vie.	Sole della mia vita.	Luz de mi vida.
(Limyair der mar vee.)	*(Soleh deh-lah mee-ah vee-tah.)*	*(Looth deh mee beedah.)*
Chérie.	Carissima.	Querida.
(Shairee.)	*(Kah-ree-see-mah.)*	*(Kehreedah.)*
Mon trésor.	Tesoro.	Preciosa.
(Mon traizawr.)	*(Teh-soro.)*	*(Prethioh-ssa.)*
Petit bout de fesse.	Dolcezza mia.	Bollito de nata.
(Ptee bood fess.)	*(Dol-cheh-tzah mee-ah.)*	*(Bohllytoh deh nátah.)*
Ma colombe.	Tortorella.	Tortolita linda.
(Mar kolombb.)	*(Tor-to-reh-lah.)*	*(Tortoleetah leendah.)*
Mon ange.	Visetto d'angelo.	Carita de angel.
(Mon ansh.)	*(Vee-seh-to d'ahn-jel-oh.)*	*(Kahreetah deh ahn-ghell.)*
Ma poupée chérie.	Fatta per amare.	Chiquita querida.
(Mar poopay shairee.)	*(Fah-tah per ah-mah-reh.)*	*(Tchickittah kehreedah.)*
Joli morceau.	Fatalona.	Tormento mío.
(Sholee morsaw.)	*(Fah-tah-lo-nah.)*	*(Torméntoh meeyoh.)*
Bath. (Ah, t'es bath, toi!)	Non plus ultra.	Gatito peludo.
(Bat (Ah, tay bat, twar!))	*(Non ploos ooltrah.)*	*(Gahteetoh pehl-loodoh.)*

RASH STATEMENTS

I yearn for you.

Ich sehne mich nach Dir.
(Ish zehne mish naach dir.)

I dream of your kisses.

Ich träume von Deinen Küssen.
(Ish troyme von dynen kussen.)

I'm crazy about you.

Ich bin ganz verrückt nach Dir.
(Ish bin gaans ferrueckt naach dir.)

Come to my arms.

Komm' in meine Arme.
(Komm in myne arme.)

I'm desperate when you are away.

Ich bin verzweifelt, wenn Du nicht bei mir bist.
(Ish bin fer-tsvyfelt, ven doo nisht by mir bist.)

You are the most beautiful girl in the world.

Du bist die schönste Frau der Welt.
(Doo bist di shoenste frao der velt.)

You are not like other women.

Du bist so ganz anders als die Anderen.
(Doo bis gans aanders aals di aanderen.)

FRENCH	ITALIAN	SPANISH
Je me consume pour vous. *(Sher mer consim poor voo.)*	Io ti bramo *(Ee-oh tee brah-moh.)*	Suspiro por tí. *(Soospeeroh pór tee.)*
Je rêve de vos (tes) baisers. *(Sher raiv der vo (tay) baizay.)*	Mi sogno i tuoi baci. *(Mee soh-nee-oh ee too-oh-ee bah-chee.)*	Sueño con tus besos. *(Swényoh kón toos bésoss.)*
Je suis fou de vous. (Vous me rendez fou.) *(Sher swee foo der voo. (Voom randay foo.))*	Sono pazzo per te. *(Soh-noh pah-tzoh per teh.)*	Estoy loco por tí. *(Stóy lókoh pór tee.)*
Viens dans mes bras! *(Vyan dan may brah!)*	Vieni nelle mie braccia. *(Vee-eh-nee nehl-leh mee-eh brah-cha.)*	Ven a mis brazos. *(Bén ah mees bráthoss.)*
Je languis loin de vous. (Je me sens perdu chaque fois que vous partez.) *(Sher languee lwan der voo. (Sherm san perdi shack fwar ker voo partay.))*	Quando non ci sei, sono disperato. *(Kwandoh non chee seh-ee, soh-noh dee-speh-rah-toh.)*	Me desespero cuando estás lejos. *(Meh desespéroh kwándoh stás léhhos.)*
Vous êtes (tu es) la plus belle fille du monde! *(Voo zait (ti ay) la pli bell feey di mond!)*	Sei la piú bella ragazza del mondo. *(Seh-ee lah pew bellah rah-gah-tzah dehl mon-doh.)*	Eres la chica más guapa del mundo. *(Éres lah cheekah máss gwáppah dél moondoh.)*
Vous n'êtes (tu n'es) pas comme les autres femmes. *(Voo nait (ti nay) par com lay zotr famm.)*	Tu sei diversa dalle altre donne. *(Too seh-ee dee-ver-sah dahl-leh altreh don-neh.)*	No eres como las demás mujeres. *(Noh éres kómoh lass dehmáss moohhéress.)*

THE BREAK

I'll write soon.

Ich schreibe bald.

(Ish shrybe baald.)

It's not going to work out is it?

Es wird wohl doch nichts mit uns, wie?

(Es vird vohl doch nishts mit oons, vi?)

We both realise it cannot last.

Es ist nicht von Dauer, das sehen wir.

(Es ist nisht fon daoer, daas zehen vir.)

I believe you have another.

Ich glaube, Du hast jemand anderen.

(Ish glaobe, doo haast yemaand aandern.)

You don't like me any more, do you?

Du hast mich nicht mehr gern, nicht wahr?

(Doo haast mish nisht mayr gairn, nisht vaar?)

Buzz off, you bore me.

Zieh' Leine. Du langweilst mich.

(Tsi' lyne, doo laangvylst mish.)

Je t'écrirai très prochainement. *(Sher teckreeray tray proshainman.)*	Scriverò presto. *(Scree-veh-ròh presto.)*	Te escribiré pronto. *(Teh screebeeréh próntoh.)*
J'ai bien peur que ça ne va pas marcher entre nous, tu crois pas? *(Shay byan pehr ker sahn va par marshay antre noo, ti crwar par?)*	Evidentemente non siamo fatti l'uno per l'altro. *(Evidenteh-mehnteh non see-amoh fah-tee l'oonoh per l'ahl-troh.)*	Esto no va a dar buen resultado, ¿verdad? *(Estoh noh báh ah dárr bwén resooltádoh, behrdád?)*
Tout comme moi, tu te rends bien compte que ça ne peut pas durer. *(Too comm mwar, tit ran byan kont ker sahn per par diray.)*	Lo sappiamo che non può durare. *(Loh sah-pee-ah-mo keh non pwo doo-rah-reh.)*	Los dos sabemos que no puede seguir. *(Lóss dóss sahbémoss ké noh pwéddeh sehgeerr.)*
Je suis persuadé que tu as quelqu'un d'autre. *(Sher swee pairsiahday ker ti ar kelkan dawtr.)*	Sento che c'è qualcun altro. *(Sent-o keh chay kwal-koon ahl-troh.)*	Creo que tienes a otro. *(Kréoh ké teeyénness ah ótroh.)*
D'ailleurs, tu ne m'aimes plus, dis-le. *(Dahyer, ti ner maim par, dee-ler.)*	Non ti piaccio piú, nevvero? *(Non tee pee-ah-cho pew, neh-vehro?)*	Ya no te gusto ¿verdad? *(Yáh noh teh goostoh, Berdath?)*
Tire-toi, tu m'embêtes! *(Teer-twar, ti mambait!)*	Vattene, mi hai stufato. *(Vah-teh-neh, me ah-y stoo-fah-to.)*	¡Lárgate! Estoy harto de ti. *(Lárgah-teh! Stóy árrtoh dé tee.)*

PROPOSING

Darling, will you marry me?

Liebling, willst Du mich heiraten?

(*Libling, villst doo mish hyraaten?*)

Will you come away with me?

Willst Du mit mir kommen?

(*Villst doo mit mir kommen?*)

Will you come and see my tattoos?

Komm' mit, ich zeige Dir meine Tätowierung.

(*Komm mit, ish tsyge dir myne taytoviroong.*)

How about it?

Wie wär's?

(*Vi vair's?*)

I have long hungered for you; may I bite you?

Ich habe so nach Dir gehungert; ich muss Dich beissen.

(*Ish haabe zo naach dir gehoongert; ish mooss dish byssen.*)

Let's make it legal.

Aber legal.

(*Aaber legaal.*)

FRENCH	ITALIAN	SPANISH
Chérie, veux-tu m'épouser? *(Shairee, ver-ti mai-poozay?)*	Tesoro, mi vuoi sposare? *(Teh-soh-roh, mee voo-oh-ee spoh-sah-reh?)*	¿Quieres casarte conmigo, querida? *(Keeyéress kahsárr-teh kón-meegoh, kehreedah?)*
Partirez-vous avec moi? *(Parteeray-voo aveck mwar?)*	Vuoi venire via con me? *(Voo-oh-ee veh-nee-reh vee-ah con meh?)*	¿Quieres marcharte conmigo? *(Keeyéress marchárteh kón-meegoh?)*
Vous venez voir mes tatouages? *(Voo vnay vwahr may tartooahsh?)*	Vuoi venire a vedere i miei tatuaggi? *(Voo-oh-ee veh-nee-reh ah veh-deh-reh ee mee-eh-ee tah-too-ah-jee?)*	¿Quieres venir, y verás mis tatuajes? *(Keeyéress behneer ee behráss miss tattooáhhess?)*
Alors? *(Alohr?)*	Che ne diresti? *(Keh neh dee-reh-stee?)*	¿Qué te parece? *(Ké teh parétheh?)*
J'ai faim de toi—je peux te mordre? *(Shay fam der twar—sher per ter mordr?)*	Ti potrei mangiare—lascia che ti dia un morsetto. *(Tee poh-treh-ee man-ja-reh—lah-shee-ah keh tee dee-ah oon mor-set-toh.)*	Tengo hambre de ti, ¿puedo morderte? *(Téngoh ámbreh dé tee, pwéddoh mohrdérr-teh?)*
On va régulariser la chose, veux-tu? *(On va raiggilareezay la shawz, ver-ti?)*	Rendiamo la cosa legale. *(Rehn-dee-ah-moh lah koh-zah leh-gah-leh.)*	Hagámoslo legal. *(Aghámoss-loh legál.)*

119

PROPOSING

Marriage is so old-fashioned, but will you give it a trial?

Heiraten ist altmodisch, aber willst Du es nicht einmal probieren?

(Hyraaten ist altmodish, aaber villst doo es nisht ynmaal probiren?)

We surely are too sensible to need a ceremony?

Eine Feier brauchen wir nicht, dazu sind wir zu vernünftig.

(Yne fyer braochen vir nisht, datsoo zind vir tsoo fernuenftig.)

When?

Wann?

(Vaann?)

IF SHE SAYS 'NO' !

Why not?

Warum nicht?

(Varoom nisht?)

Don't be old-fashioned.

Sei doch nicht so altmodisch.

(Zy doch nisht zo altmodish.)

FRENCH	ITALIAN	SPANISH
Le mariage est une institution démodée, je sais bien, mais si on essayait un peu? *(Ler mareeahsh aitin ansteetisyon daimoday, sher say byan, may see on essaiyay an per?)*	Il matrimonio è un'istituzione antiquata, ma vuoi fare una prova? *(Eel mah-tree-moh-nee-oh eh oon ee-stee-too-tzee-ohneh antee-kwah-tah, mah voo-oh-eee fah-reh oo-nah pro-vah?)*	Casarse está pasado de moda, pero podríamos hacer un ensayo. *(Kasárr-seh stáh passádoh deh módah, péroh podreeyamoss athérr oon ensáhyoh.)*
Nous sommes bien trop raisonnables pour avoir besoin d'une cérémonie, n'est-ce pas? *(Noo somm byan tro raizonabl poor avwahr berzwan din sairaimonee, naice-par?)*	Ma siamo persone troppo intelligenti per avere bisogno di una cerimonia. *(Mah see-ah-moh per-sohneh trop-poh intel-lee-jehntee per ah-ver bee-zoh-neeoh dee oo-nah chairee-mohnee-ah.)*	Somos demasiado sensibles para necesitar una ceremonia. *(Sómoss demmasyádoh senseeb-less párah nethessittárr oonah zerehmón-yah.)*
Quand? *(Kan?)*	Quando? *(Kwan-doh?)*	¿Cuándo? *(Kwándoh?)*
Pourquoi pas? *(Poorkwar par?)*	Perchè no? *(Per-keh noh?)*	¿Por qué no? *(Pór ké noh?)*
Qu'est-ce que tu peux être vieux jeu!!! *(Kaisker ti per zaitr vyer sher!!!)*	Non essere così all'antica. *(Non ehs-seh-reh koh-zée ahl-lan-tee-kah.)*	¡No seas anticuada! *(Noh sé-ass antikwádda!)*

IF SHE SAYS 'NO' !

Everybody else does.	Jeder macht es doch so. *(Yeder maacht es doch zo.)*
Nobody will know.	Braucht doch niemand zu wissen. *(Braocht doch nimaant tsoo vissen.)*
The place is empty.	Est ist kein Mensch hier. *(Es ist kyn mensh hir.)*
Don't torment me.	Quäle mich nicht. *(Quayle mish nisht.)*
But I *do* love you.	Aber ich liebe Dich doch. *(Aaber ish lihbe dish doch.)*

REASONS

I can't marry you, my wife would object.	Ich kann Dich nicht heiraten, meine Frau würde es nicht erlauben. *(Ish kann dish nisht hyraaten, myne frao vuerde es nisht erlaoben.)*

FRENCH	ITALIAN	SPANISH
Tout le monde le fait.	Lo fanno tutti.	Todo el mundo lo hace.
(Tool mond ler fay.)	*(Loh fahn-noh toot-tee.)*	*(Tóddoh él moondoh loh átheh.)*
Personne n'en saura rien.	Non lo saprà nessuno.	Nadie lo sabrá.
(Pairsonn nan sawrah ryan.)	*(Non loh sah-práh nehs-soo-noh.)*	*(Náddye loh sahbráh.)*
Il n'y a personne ici.	Non c'è nessuno.	Este lugar está desierto.
(Eel nyar pairsonn eecee.)	*(Non-chèh nes-soo-noh.)*	*(Ésteh loogárr stáh dessyértoh.)*
Ne me tourmente pas.	Non tormentarmi.	No me atormentes más.
(Ner mer toormant par.)	*(Non tor-mentar-mee.)*	*(Noh mé attorméntess máss.)*
Mais *bien sûr* que je t'aime!	Ma sí che ti amo.	Pero es que te amo.
(May byan sir kersh taim!)	*(Mah seè keh tee ah-moh.)*	*(Péroh ess ké teh ámoh.)*
Je ne peux pas t'épouser, ma femme n'aimerait pas du tout ça!	Non posso sposarti, mia moglie sarebbe contraria.	No puedo casarme contigo, porque mi esposa se opondría.
(Shern per par taipoozay, ma famm naimray par di too sah!)	*(Non po-soh spo-sahr-tee, mee-ah mo-lee-eh sah-rehbbeh con-trah-ree-ah.)*	*(Nó pwéddoh kassárr-meh kón-teegoh, pór-ké mee spóssah sé ohpóndreeyah.)*

REASONS

I can't marry you because I am too young.

Ich kann Dich nicht heiraten, weil ich zu jung bin.

(Ish kann dish nisht hyraaten, vyl ish tsoo yoong bin.)

I can't marry you because I am a fugitive.

Ich kann Dich nicht heiraten, ich bin flüchtig.

(Ish kann dish nisht hyraaten, ish bin flueshtig.)

I can't marry you because I am under age.

Ich kann Dich nicht heiraten, weil ich noch unmündig bin.

(Ish kann dish nisht hyraaten, vyl ish noch oonmuendig bin.)

I can't marry you, because of my war wound.

Ich kann Dich nicht heiraten wegen meiner Kriegsverletzung.

(Ish kann dish nisht hyraaten vegen myner kriegsferletsung.)

I can't marry you because I am too poor.

Ich kann Dich nicht heiraten, weil ich zu arm bin.

(Ish kann dish nisht hyraaten, vyl ish tsoo arm bin.)

FRENCH	ITALIAN	SPANISH
Je ne peux pas t'épouser, je suis trop jeune. *(Shern per par taipoozay, sher swee tro shern.)*	Non posso sposarti, sono troppo giovane. *(Non po-soh spo-sahr-tee, sono tro-poh joh-vah-neh.)*	No puedo casarme contigo porque soy demasiado joven. *(Nó pwéddoh kassárr-meh kón-teegoh, pór-ké sóy dehmassyadoh hóbben.)*
Je ne peux pas t'épouser, je suis en fuite pour l'instant. *(Shern per par taipoozay, sher sweezan fweet poor lanstan.)*	Non posso sposarti, sono un evaso. *(Non po-soh spo-sahr-tee, sono oon eh-vah-so.)*	No puedo casarme contigo porque soy un fugitivo. *(Nó pwéddoh kassárr-meh kón-teegoh, pór-ké sóy oon foohheetiboh.)*
Tu ne peux pas épouser un mineur que je sache! *(Tin per par zaipoozay an meenehr ker sher sash!)*	Non posso sposarti, sono minorenne. *(Non po-soh spo-sahr-tee, sono mee-noh-reh-neh.)*	No puedo casarme contigo porque soy menor de edad. *(Nó pwéddoh kassárr-meh kón-teegoh, pór-ké sóy mehnórr deh eddád.)*
Il m'est impossible de t'épouser à cause de mes blessures de guerre. *(Eel may tamposeebl der taipoozay ar cawz der may blessir der gair.)*	Non posso sposarti a causa della mia ferita di guerra. *(Non po soh spo-sahr-tee, ah cah-oo-sah-deh-lah mee-a feh-ree-tah dee gweh-rah.)*	No puedo casarme contigo por mi herida de guerra. *(Nó pwéddoh kassárr-meh kón-teegoh, pór mee ehreedah deh ghérrah.)*
Je ne peux pas t'épouser, je suis trop pauvre. *(Shern per par taipoozay, sher swee tro pawvr.)*	Non posso sposarti, sono troppo povero. *(Non po-soh spo-sahr-tee, sono tro-poh poh-veh-ro.)*	No puedo casarme contigo porque soy demasiado pobre. *(Nó pwéddoh kassárr-meh kón-teegoh, pór-ké sóy dehmassyádoh póbbreh.)*

SOME USEFUL WORDS

Ravishing.

Hinreissend.
(Hinryssend.)

Beautiful.

Schön.
(Shoen.)

Bed.

Bett.
(Bett.)

Lovely.

Reizend.
(Rytsend.)

Exquisite.

Grosse Klasse.
(Grosse klasse.)

Settee.

Sofa.
(Zofa.)

Superb.

Hervorragend.
(Herfor-raagend.)

Dazzling.

Verwirrend.
(Fervirrend.)

Chaise-longue.

Chaise-longue.
(Chaise-longue.)

FRENCH	ITALIAN	SPANISH
Ravissant. (Raveesant.)	Affascinante. (Ah-fah-shee-nahn-teh.)	Arrebatadora. (Ahrrehbahtahdórah.)
Beau (Belle) (Bo (Bell).)	Bella. (Beh-llah.)	Hermosa. (Ehrmóssah.)
Un lit. (An lee.)	Letto. (Leh-to.)	Cama. (Kámah.)
Mignon (Mignonne). (Meenyonn.)	Incantevole. (In-cahn-teh-voleh.)	Cariñosa. (Karynyóssa.)
Exquis (Exquise). (Exkee (Exkeez).)	Deliziosa. (Deh-lee-tzeeo-sah.)	Exquisita. (Exkeeseetah.)
Un divan. (An deevan.)	Sofá. (Sofah.)	Sofá. (Sofah.)
Superbe. (Sipairb.)	Meravigliosa. (Meh-rah-vee-lee-o-sah.)	Soberbia. (Sobérbeeyah.)
Eblouissant (Eblouissante). (Ebblweesan (Ebblweesant).)	Splendente. (Splehn-dehnteh.)	Deslumbrante. (Dessloombránteh.)
Un récamier. (An recahmyay.)	Sedia a sdraio. (Seh-deeah ah sdřah-yo.)	Tumbona. (Toombónah.)